MAN[illegible] OBS

By the same author

THE REALITY OF MANAGEMENT
*THE REALITY OF ORGANIZATIONS
*HOW COMPUTERS AFFECT MANAGEMENT
CONTRASTS IN MANAGEMENT
CHOICES FOR THE MANAGER
THE BOSS: The Life and Times of the British Businessman (*with Roy Lewis*)
THE DISTRICT ADMINISTRATOR IN THE NATIONAL HEALTH SERVICE
(*with Peter Smith, Jenny Blake and Pauline Wingate*)

*Also published by Macmillan

Managers and their Jobs

A Study of the Similarities and Differences in the Ways Managers Spend their Time

Rosemary Stewart

Second Edition

MACMILLAN
PRESS

First edition 1967
Second edition 1988

Published by
THE MACMILLAN PRESS LTD
Houndmills, Basingstoke, Hampshire RG21 2XS
and London
Companies and representatives
throughout the world

Printed in Hong Kong

British Library Cataloguing in Publication Data
Stewart, Rosemary
Managers and their jobs: a study of the similarities and differences in the ways managers spend their time.—2nd ed.
1. Comparative management
I. Title
658.4 HD38
ISBN 0–333–45592–4 (hardcover)
ISBN 0–333–45593–2 (paperback)

Contents

List of Figures

Diaries

Acknowledgements

I am most grateful to all those whose cooperation made this work possible. My first thanks are to the Nuffield Foundation, which kindly financed the main research. I should particularly like to thank the managers who kept the diaries, both at the pilot stage and in the main research. I much appreciated the help of the Institute of Marketing and Sales Management, the Institution of Works Managers, the Institution of Production Engineers and the Institute of Cost and Works Accountants in obtaining volunteers from among their members. I am grateful to the companies who allowed me to try out pilot versions of the diary at their management courses, and to the personnel managers who obtained volunteers from their companies to take part in the research. I should also like to thank those responsible for the computer work: the Atlas Computer Laboratory of the Science Research Council, who did all the computer work except that contained in Chapter 6; Mr Nigel Howard, who was my colleague at the London School of Economics, for the use of his programme for classifying the managers into different job types; and the University of London Atlas Computing Service for the computer work on the classification.

I am especially grateful to Miss Janet Worrall and to Mr R. G. Stansfield, who very kindly read the book in manuscript and pointed out passages where I had been obscure, or where I had unduly maltreated the English language. They naturally bear no responsibility for the defects that remain. I should also like to thank Mrs J. Johnson for her cheerful thoroughness in checking the tabulations and for the keen interest she showed throughout, and Miss Margaret Symons for her care in typing the final manuscript, and Miss Denise Lacey for her cheerful and efficient help in preparing the manuscript for the second edition.

ROSEMARY STEWART

Introduction to the First Edition

What do managers do?[1] Managers have three reasons for being interested in the answer to this question. The first is because it can help them in thinking about their own work and how they do it. The second is because more knowledge of the characteristics of different management jobs will be useful to them in trying to plan their future career. The third reason is that a better understanding of the jobs done by subordinates will make it easier to select and train them successfully.

What do managers need to know about their own job and how they do it? Some will answer: 'Nothing that I do not know already'. They are likely to be people who are impatient of analysis, who believe that good managers are born and need no training to improve their skills as a manager. Others will say that they would like to know both how they really spend their time and how they ought to spend it. They want to answer the question: 'Am I working as efficiently as possible?' It is a difficult question for managers to try to answer for themselves, caught up, as so many managers are, in a nearly continuous series of discussions, interruptions and crises. This book, and especially Chapter 9, can help those who want to answer that question.

Once managers begin to think about the nature of their jobs, they may ask themselves how their job differs from that of their colleagues. What are the special problems associated with each job? What kind of people are most suited to the different jobs? Looking at posts to which they might aspire, they may ask which would suit them best. They may find it difficult to answer that question as they know so little about the characteristics of these jobs. At this point they may – but probably will not – turn to the management literature for guidance. If they do they will find a discussion of the manager's job. They will read about the characteristics common to all managers' jobs: planning, organising, motivating and controlling. But they will find little or nothing that will help them to understand the particular features of their own or other jobs; nothing about how the job of a works manager differs either from that of a sales manager, or from that of a research manager.

This book is based on research that sought to explore some of the differences as well as some of the similarities between managers' jobs. The research aimed to distinguish different kinds of jobs and to describe their special characteristics and problems. It was made possible by the cooperation of 160 middle and senior managers who were interested in finding out how they spent their time by keeping a specially designed diary for four weeks.

Managers and their Jobs is addressed to managers who are interested in organising their time more efficiently, to all those who are concerned with management development, and to research workers, and managers who are interested in the study of management behaviour.

Chapter 1 discusses briefly the different questions that people have asked about the nature of managers' work and the kind of answers that they have given. It describes the previous research that has been done to answer the question, 'How do managers spend their time?' It then outlines the aim and methods of the research on which this book is based.

Chapters 2 to 5 describe how the 160 managers spent their time. Diagrams show both the way in which the managers spent their time on average, and how great were the variations from the average. The reasons for these wide variations are discussed. Chapter 6 classifies the managers into five job types on the basis of similarities in their work activities and contacts. Chapter 7 discusses the implications of job types for the selection and training of managers. It suggests that certain jobs may tend to produce characteristic inefficiencies, in the same way as the holders of certain jobs may be prone to particular illnesses.

Chapter 8, on 'Lessons for the Manager', describes how managers can analyse the way in which they work. It gives a list of questions that managers should ask themselves, to assess how effectively they use their time. It discusses some of the ways in which managers may work inefficiently. Readers who are principally interested in improving their own efficiency should start the book at the last chapter.

1967 ROSEMARY STEWART

Introduction to the Second Edition

The study on which this book is based is still relevant to understanding what managers do, and of use to managers wanting to manage their time better. It remains of interest for a number of reasons: it is one of the largest and most carefully designed studies; it covers a variety of middle and senior managers; and, unlike later studies, it shows the variation in what managers do both between managers, and for the same manager over four weeks. Each figure shows the average time for the 160 managers studied and the range of distribution.

There were two aims in preparing this new edition. The first was to place the study in the perspective of forty years of research into what managers do. The second was to strengthen the utility of the book for managers who want to improve their effectiveness and for those who seek to help them to do so. Studies undertaken since the first edition, especially those by Kotter, Mintzberg and by the author, have used other methods and contributed new insights to our understanding of what managers do. These are discussed in a new chapter, Chapter 8 on What *Do* Managers Do?, together with their implications for the manager. The discussion of early studies in Chapter 1 is now shorter.

Since first writing this book the author has spent much of her time working with managers to help them to understand their jobs, to review the effectiveness of their approach, and to manage their time better. This experience has led to changes in the last chapter on 'Too Little Time? How to Help Yourself'.

Chapters 2 to 7 which describe the research and the implications of job types remain the same, except for a few additions which are mainly to give more emphasis to individual variations. The experience and knowledge of later work points to the need for this shift of emphasis. In the first edition not enough importance was attached to the influence of individual variations as an explanation of differences in the way that the sample managers spent their time. The writer's later observational studies of managers in similar jobs showed how greatly individuals can differ in the work that they do. This difference is greater in some jobs than in others, but the possibility exists in all.

The second edition, like the first, is addressed to managers who are interested in organising their time more efficiently, and to all those who can benefit from a better understanding of the nature and diversity of managerial work. This should include those concerned with management education and development. This edition also provides a quarry for students who want to compare the work pattern of current managers with those of twenty years ago, as well as for those who want to explore one of the many ideas put forward, such as inspection as a commonly displaced activity.

All the managers who took part in this study were men, hence the use of 'he' in all the chapters about the research results. In a comparable study today one would expect to find some women. Otherwise in this second edition account is taken of objections to the use of the male pronoun by various changes including the occasional use of 'she' rather than 'he'.

1988 ROSEMARY STEWART

1 Studying What Managers Do

This chapter is primarily for those with a professional interest in understanding the nature of managers' jobs. This should include human resource managers and management trainers, but other managers may prefer to start at Chapter 2 after reading the summary of this chapter. Those who want more information about how the research, on which this book is based, was carried out should turn to p. 7.

The problem is to decide what aspects of managers' activities to study. Some of the questions that might be asked about a managerial job are listed below, together with why the answers could be useful.

WHAT QUESTIONS SHOULD ONE ASK?

(i) How specialised is the job?

Specialisation is usually thought of in terms of subject matter: the more restricted the subject matter, the more specialised is the job. Another aspect of the amount of specialisation in a job, which is rarely considered, is that of the range of contacts that it involves. A job that is very specialised in its subject matter may have a wide variety of contacts.

Information on the amount of specialisation could be useful for three reasons. First, it could show the range of knowledge that the job-holder would need; for instance, would some knowledge of accountancy be essential, useful, or irrelevant? Second, it could show whether the job was likely to be a good training ground for those senior posts that require a broad understanding of the business. Third, it would probably tell us something about the qualities of leadership needed in the job. The leadership of subordinates in a very specialised department will be based, at least in part, on superior knowledge or experience.

(ii) What kind of contacts does the job involve?

The title of the job, and its position on an organisation chart, may provide no indication of the range of contacts. A job may involve contacts with people at the same level in a variety of other departments. Such a job could be said to have wide horizontal contacts. Another job, and sometimes even the same job, may require contacts with those at several levels above and below the manager's own position in the hierarchy. Such a job can be described as having a long vertical range of contacts. Then there are jobs that require a wide range of external contacts. Most large organisations have some jobs that provide a much greater variety of contacts than other jobs at the same level – a fact that ambitious young managers soon discover. Such jobs can be useful for training those with promotion potential. These are bridging jobs, as they bring their holders into contact with some of the problems and personalities in other departments and at levels of more than one remove. The management development department needs to be aware of such jobs in the organisation, and of the special advantages which they can give their holders both in understanding different parts of the organisation and in being noticed by senior managers outside their own departments.

A knowledge of the type and range of contacts associated with particular jobs can also be useful for training. Training in communications is part of many post-experience courses, but attention is seldom paid to the different types of communication that different jobs may involve. The problems of communicating effectively will vary with the following factors: the relative levels of those concerned; the degree of common understanding of the subject; the extent to which those involved have a common background; the relationship that exists between them; and the extent to which they do or do not agree about work objectives.

(iii) What form do most of the contacts take?

Some jobs involve mainly face-to-face contacts; in others the telephone is an important means of communication. In some jobs the manager will spend much of the time in committees or in informal group discussions. Different forms of contact require different skills, which may have to be learned. The art of chairing a meeting, for example, is one that few managers can master without experience.

(iv) What type of work pattern does the job tend to impose?

Jobs have different work patterns. The work pattern of a job is shown by the duration of its activities, by the extent to which its occupant can hope to plan the use of time, by the number and frequency of interruptions and by the extent to which activities repeat themselves. Some jobs are much more fragmented than others; some are subject to much greater time pressure than others. One can distinguish, at one extreme, a job that permits the manager to plan the day or the week with a reasonable chance of being able to keep to the plan, and, at the other extreme, a job where what happens each day is largely determined by other people. In the former the manager may spend an hour or more on one activity. In the latter, the day is likely to consist mainly of short episodes. A knowledge of the pattern of a job can show some of the pressures that the job imposes upon its holder. Such information can be useful both in selection and in training. In selection it can help in eliminating those who would not stand the pressures that can be imposed by a very fragmented job, or by one subject to great time pressures. In training, such knowledge can be used to help the manager to surmount the particular pressures of the job.

(v) What kind of decisions does the job involve?

This question has multiple answers, depending on what aspects of decision-taking are being considered. Decisions vary in many ways: in the kind of knowledge that is required; in the amount of information that is available; in the standard of judgement that is needed; and in the degree of uncertainty that there is about the correctness of the decision. Decisions also vary in their importance for the success of the enterprise. The decision process may be a short-term one; many jobs only necessitate that kind of decision. The decision process may also be long-term and discontinuous. This is true of many of the more important decisions. The time pressure to make a decision also varies. Some decisions require moral courage, particularly those that affect other people.

A knowledge of the kind of decisions that have to be made in particular jobs would help in selection by showing what knowledge and experience is required, and, for some decisions, what kind of temperamental and moral character. Such knowledge is relevant to training for promotion.

(vi) What are the main methods of communication?

All managers' jobs involve discussions, but in some jobs they may occupy nearly all the working day. In a few paperwork may take up nearly as much time. This may seem too simple an analysis to tell us anything of interest about a manager's job, but the proportion of time that a manager spends in discussions can show how rapid is the rate of change and how important persuasion is as an aspect of the job. Such an analysis can also tell us something about the kind of temperament needed for the job. Increasingly some jobs require a facility with electronic forms of communication.

(vii) How much variety and what kind is provided by the job?

Jobs vary in different ways. Some have a regular monthly or seasonal cycle. Others have a similar pattern each week with only minor variations. Yet others have little routine as the problems with which they have to deal change frequently. Different aspects of the job may vary such as the place of work, the people contacted, the tempo of work and its content.

A picture of the ways in which a job may vary from day to day, from week to week or over a longer period, can help to give a clearer idea of the nature of the job. It can show the kind of adaptation that is required. It can show too some of the stresses in the job as well as some of the interest. It can indicate whether it is the kind of job that will provide a challenge for a long time and thus help a manager to develop, or whether it is one that an able man or woman should not hold for long because of its limited variety.

METHODS OF STUDYING HOW MANAGERS SPEND THEIR TIME

A study of the use of time is simpler, both conceptually and methodologically, than a study of what managers do. Even so there are decisions to be made about the methods to use and about the content that is possible with those methods. Three main methods have been used by research workers. The first is to ask managers to estimate how they divide their time between different activities. The second is for managers to keep a record themselves. The third is for an observer to record what the manager does. All three methods require considerable care in deciding what categories to use for analysis.

The first method has a number of advantages over the other two. It is much the simplest. It is easier to get managers to cooperate since cooperation will take little time. It is also a method that can be used at training courses, where there are subjects readily available. More willing cooperation makes it possible to select the sample in the expectation that most will agree to take part. The analysis of the material is much quicker as there is only one set of figures for each manager – a time estimate for each heading. Because of these various advantages the method can be used much more easily to study large numbers than the other two methods, which are more costly and time-consuming.

The first method suffers from the great disadvantage that people's estimates of how they spend their time may be wrong and the research worker may not be able to judge how far they are wrong, or in what direction. Considerable differences between the estimated and recorded time for some activities have been shown when the two have been compared in a number of studies.[1] Because of the limitations of the first method it was superseded in later studies by other methods.

The second method is self-recording using a diary and the third is observation. Both are likely to be more reliable than self-estimates, and also have the advantage that they can show variations in how individuals spend their time. They have the disadvantage that they are more time-consuming for the research worker and make greater demands on the individuals being studied.

The main advantages of the diary method compared with observation are:

1. It is less time-consuming, less expensive and much less restricted in locality. Hence many more managers can be studied over a wider area of industry and locality.
2. The length of study is less restricted; with observation the longer the period the fewer the number of people that can be studied.
3. Classification is made by those who know what they are doing. For some types of analysis the observer would have to ask them to explain their actions.
4. All time can be recorded, whereas an observer may be excluded from confidential discussions.

The main disadvantage of diaries is that they greatly limit both the scope and content of what can be studied. The scope is limited because the manager cannot devote much time to the recording, and the content because it is difficult to get managers to record in the same way if the item being recorded allows much scope for differences in interpretation.

The main advantages of observation compared with diary-keeping are:

1. The observer has time to make more detailed and comprehensive recordings.
2. The record is likely to be more complete and the observer is much less likely to omit a recording through pressure of work.
3. A consistent standard can be used for recording the activities of different people.

Both self-recording and observation can either aim to cover the whole period under review, or use the incident method of recording, by sampling at random intervals. This means that the manager, or the observer, records what the manager is doing at random intervals throughout the day. The incident method is more economical of time and money than recording the whole period, whether by using a diary or by an observer. It imposes less of a burden on the manager than a continuous diary, and avoids the constant presence of an observer. The incident method is especially useful for an observer as it enables more people to be studied. It is most useful where all those to be studied are, and remain, under one roof, so that the observer can keep in touch with them. The incident method limits observations to those activities that can be immediately interpreted, since the observer may find it more difficult to understand what is happening when observing for brief periods. This method can be used with self-recording if there is a random alarm for telling the manager when to make a record. The proportion of time spent in particular activities can be estimated by the incident method, but it cannot give information about the duration of the individual incident.

AIMS AND METHODS OF THIS STUDY

Aims

The main aim of this research was to discover some of the similarities and differences in the ways in which managers spend their time. The aim was to discover differences between jobs rather than between individuals, following the evidence from the Ohio State University studies that the nature of the job helps to determine what its holder will do.[2] Related to the main aim was a further one of trying to distinguish different job-types on the basis of the ways in which their holders spend their time. Yet another aim was to discover some of the ways in which managers may use their time inefficiently.

It was hoped that a study of the differences between managers' jobs might show ways in which the selection and training of managers could be improved. Information about such differences could influence both the content of courses and the decisions on who should attend them. Courses are usually designed for different levels of management: a study of how managers spend their time might show that some other basis for deciding on the composition of a course would be more useful.

More knowledge about the differences between jobs and hence about the kind of experience obtained in different jobs could also influence career planning. Finally, it was hoped that information about the ways in which managers work inefficiently could be of use in management development.

Methods

Two main measures can be used of a manager's activities. One is the amount of time spent on particular activities. The other is the frequency with which something is done. For many purposes time is the more comprehensive measure, but for some, frequency may be the better measure. Sometimes a combination of the two will be desirable. One may, for instance, want to know both how long a manager spends with subordinates and how frequently they are seen. Time was the main measure used in previous studies. It is also the main measure used in the study described in this book, but frequency is used for some aspects of the managers' work.

Designing the diary

The diary method was chosen instead of observation because the research aimed to study more than 100 managers in a large number of different companies. This aim could not be achieved by observation without a large team of observers. The first, pilot, stage of the research was the exploration of different types of diaries for recording managers' activities. Two series of seminars were held for managers, each for one afternoon a week for nine weeks. Those attending ranged from junior to senior management and had jobs in different functions. They also came from companies of different sizes and industries. Members of the seminar kept different types of diaries between each meeting and at the seminar discussed their usefulness, ease of recording and reliability.[3] After the seminars a revised diary was tried out on members of middle management courses in three organisations. The managers kept the diary for a month before coming to the course and discussed it at the course. This diary was again revised and tried out at another course. These repeated discussions with more than fifty managers of how they had used the diary and what they thought of it, together with a comparison of the completed diaries, helped to show how the diaries were being kept in practice and where the recordings might be unreliable.

The main conclusions from these experiments with different types of diaries was that only simple, easily defined information can be collected if the information is to be comparable. In particular the kinds of action classification used in earlier studies was shown to be very unreliable. It is not difficult for a manager to be reasonably consistent in classifying his own work under such headings as 'getting information' or 'planning', but the discussions at the seminar and at the courses showed wide differences in what people understood by such terms. Even when the terms were defined, differences in interpretation persisted. It was therefore decided to exclude a classification of kinds of action, such as planning or giving information, from the main diary.

A copy of the diary used in the main research is given in Appendix I. It is much simpler than the first ones that were tried out in the seminar. The information obtained from this diary is discussed in the next six chapters. The diary was designed to record the place of work, whether the manager was alone, with one other person or with two or more people, and with whom the work was being done. The diary also recorded how the time was divided between such easily classified activities as inspection (a personal tour of work-place) and telephoning. As the discussion in the seminars had shown that it was difficult to distinguish between the reading of company material, writing and dictating, these were lumped together under 'writing and internal reading'. There was a section headed 'What' which listed the main functions such as sales and production.

The diary was also designed to show the extent to which the manager's day was fragmented. One measure of this was the number of fleeting contacts, both personal and by telephone, of under five minutes. These fleeting contacts were recorded in a separate section at the bottom of each page. This section of the diary differed from the rest in two ways. First, the number of such contacts were counted – not their total time, because hard-pressed managers could not be expected to keep an accurate record of periods of under five minutes. Second, more than one fleeting contact could be recorded on the same page. The reason for these two differences in diary design was to make it easier for managers to record as many of their fleeting contacts as they could.

Earlier in this chapter we listed some of the questions that should be asked if one wants to study what managers do. There were seven questions:

1. How specialised is the job?
2. What kind of contacts does the job involve?
3. What form do most of the contacts take?
4. What kind of work pattern does the job tend to impose?
5. What kind of decisions does the job involve?
6. How much time is spent on different kinds of activity?
7. How much, and what kinds of, variety are provided by the job?

This study can give answers to questions 2 to 4 for the sample of 160 managers. It gives some information on questions 1, 6, and 7, but none about question 5. The pilot-study tried out different diaries for recording decisions, but no record of decisions was included in the main research. This was partly because of the difficulties of designing a satisfactory form for analysing decisions, and partly because of the danger of overloading the managers who volunteered to take part in the research.

The main diary, which was filled in by ticks, was supplemented by two other forms. The first asked the manager to describe each day the three activities that had taken up the greatest amount of time. This gave some information about the content of the work. The second form, which was filled in weekly, asked questions that were designed to check on how well the manager had kept the diary. One question was 'How often did you fill in the diary?' and another was 'What was the longest time interval that elapsed before you completed the diary?' The managers had been asked to complete the diary after each incident and those whose answers to these questions were unsatisfactory were excluded from the final analysis. Managers were also asked whether the week had been abnormal and, if so, in what ways.

The pilot-studies showed that there might be considerable variations in the record of a manager's work from week to week. It was clear that one or two weeks were unlikely to be long enough to give a good picture of what the manager was doing. It was therefore decided to ask managers to keep the diary for four weeks. This period was chosen as it seemed to be the best compromise between a sufficient period time to show up variations in the job, and the maximum length of time that one could hope the managers would retain their interest and continue to keep the diary carefully. Experience suggested that some managers would have been willing to go on beyond four weeks, but that the interest of most would flag. The choice of the four-week period was left to the individual manager who was asked to choose a period, by a certain date, that would be representative of the normal work.

Written follow-up

All the cooperating managers were sent details of the way in which they had spent their time, together with comparative figures for managers in similar jobs. They were then asked to comment on any unusual features in their figures. Some of them gave very detailed answers, which provided another source of material that could be used in interpreting the diary data and in trying to explain individual and contextual reasons for unusual figures.

The sample

The goal set was a minimum of 100 managers with a maximum of 200. The lower limit was felt to be the minimum for exploring some of the differences between a variety of jobs. The upper limit was determined by the demands on computer time – in those early days when even a researcher on a small project like this one had to take that into account. Since the aim was to study differences as well as similarities in managers' jobs, the sample should include managers in different types of jobs. It was decided to try to get the main part of the sample from senior sales and marketing, production and accounting managers in a variety of companies. This would enable comparisons to be made both between managers in similar jobs in different organisations and between managers in the three main functions. It was also hoped to make some vertical comparisons within a few companies, and to include some more specialist managers. It was essential that managers should want to cooperate, so that they would be willing to maintain the diary-keeping for the four weeks. Volunteers who had the right kind of jobs were, therefore, invited in the hope that enough would respond.

This book discusses the work activities of 160 managers, who kept the diaries for four weeks. Another thirty-odd managers kept diaries, but either did not complete the four weeks because of illness, change of job or lack of interest, or did not fill them in regularly or reliably enough. Many more, particularly sales managers, said that they would keep the diary after they had seen a copy, but did not do so.

The sample was obtained in two main ways. The first was to ask some of the professional management bodies for help in enlisting the cooperation of some of their members. The Institution of Works Managers, the Institute of Marketing and Sales Management and the Institute of Cost and Works Accountants were approached, to find volunteers from the three main functions of production, marketing and sales and finance. The Institution of Production Engineers was approached, to obtain a more specialist group of managers. All these bodies very kindly agreed to help. The IMSM and IPE both approached a random sample of their full members. The other two bodies published information in their journal about the research, which invited cooperation. Those members who showed interest were sent a sample diary to see whether they still wished to cooperate. This approach to the Institutions produced middle and senior managers, including some general managers, in companies in many different manufacturing industries. It also brought volunteers from five managers who were not in a manufacturing industry. The companies ranged in size from 12 to over 30 000 employees.

The second way of obtaining managers who were willing to keep a diary was to ask the personnel managers of some large manufacturing companies whether they could obtain a cross-section of managers in one department or of managers in different departments at the same level. The aim here was to compare jobs in the same department, or on the same level, within one company. Those who were willing to help had difficulty in getting people to cooperate. In all, about sixty managers were obtained in this way. The second approach produced middle and senior managers and two junior managers. Both approaches brought one or two volunteers from those holding specialist posts who had few or no subordinates. These were included as they held jobs that required them to work closely with other people.

The sample, therefore, covers a wide variety of middle and senior managers' jobs in sales and production with a smaller number of accountants and company secretaries. It includes some specialist managers in engineering and in research. It also includes some of the jobs that are found only in very large companies. The second method of obtaining volunteers, by approaching the personnel managers of large companies, means that the sample includes a disproportionately large number of managers from big companies. It is not a random sample as the managers were volunteers and it was not possible to specify, except within broad categories, who the volunteers should be. It is also clearly not a representatie sample, but then we do not know what would be a representative sample of British management. An analysis of the sample by function, level, industry, size of company and geographical location is given in Appendices II and III. This information was obtained from a questionnaire completed by all the managers.

The analysis of the diaries

(i) *Reliability* The discussions held in the different management courses had shown some possible sources of unreliability. These were taken into account in designing the final diary. There were also checks on the accuracy of the individual diaries. Each page of each diary was examined before it was sent to the computer-centre to check that it was completed satisfactorily. Some diaries were rejected at this stage. Others were rejected after reading the weekly comment sheet which indicated that they had not been kept regularly enough. Even with these precautions it is likely that some of the managers did not record everything that they should have done. This is most likely to have happened when they were especially busy, and is most likely to have led to their not recording some of their fleeting contacts.

It is not possible to say whether the managers consciously or unconsciously biased their entries in order to give a particular picture of the way they worked, but a number of precautions were taken to try to ensure that they had no reasons for doing so. They were not asked to estimate how they spent their time, for fear that this might bias their recording. The content of the diary was neutral so that there were no obvious reasons for misrecording, with the possible exception of the length of working hours. This apparently did not deter some people from recording very short hours. One safeguard against bias was that the managers were interested in obtaining a picture of how they spend their time, which they could then compare with that for managers in similar jobs. This should have been an incentive to record their time accurately. Another safeguard was that the managers were anonymous, each being given a code number in the analysis.

In spite of the care taken in the diary design, two parts of the diary still proved to be unreliable. One was the distinction in the section for fleeting contacts between those that were interruptions and those that were not. Inspection of the diaries showed that some managers had not made this distinction, so it could not be used in the general analysis. The other section that proved unreliable was the one under the heading 'What' with subheadings for different functions such as sales or production. This was the only part of the diary that attempted to analyse the content of the work. Analysis of the completed diaries, along with the detailed information about the manager's job and the daily diary sheet describing the main activities, showed that some managers had used the classification 'general management' much more than others. The aim of including this section under 'What' had been to distinguish how much time managers spent in their own function, as a guide to the degree of specialisation of their jobs. Unfortunately, because of the different interpretations of classifying their work under 'What', little use could be made of this part of the diary material. The 'What' section of the diary provided only two of the twenty-five variables used for classifying managers into different groups. The variables are described in Appendix IV.

(ii) *Computer analysis* The computer analysis was in two parts. The first and longer part, which was carried out at the Atlas Computer Laboratory of the Science Research Council, was the addition and cross-tabulation of the different entries. The average number of diary pages used by each of the 160 managers was 257. Each page had a minimum of five entries on it so there was a large quantity of simple addition to be done. The computer produced the time that each manager had spent each week under each heading, and the total for the four weeks. It also gave the cross-tabulations between a lot of the headings and some other computations. The information coming from the computer was cross-checked for human errors in handling the material for the computer. The second part of the computer analysis was done at the Atlas Computer at London University, where there was a suitable programme, which is described in Chapter 7 and in Appendix IV. It produced the cluster analysis which divided the managers into different groups.

SUMMARY

What do managers do? This is a more complex question than 'how do managers spend their time?' Even this apparently simple question is too complex to be studied until it is broken down into a number of separate questions about different aspects of managers' work. Seven such questions are described.

Three methods have been used in different studies of the way managers spend their time. The first is to ask managers to estimate how they spend their time; the second is observation by the research worker; the third is self-recording, using a diary. The advantages and disadvantages of each method are discussed.

The main aim of the research on which this book is based was to analyse the similarities and differences in the ways in which managers spend their time. The emphasis was on job, rather than individual, differences. A related aim was to classify managers' jobs on the basis of these differences. A further aim was to try to discover some of the ways in which managers may use their time inefficiently.

A long pilot-study investigated different types of diary. One problem was to try to ensure that the material collected in diaries, which were completed by different managers, would be comparable. This meant that there must be no major differences in interpretation. A classification of kinds of actions under such headings as planning, or giving information, did not pass this test. The final diary was, therefore, based on simple activities that could be clearly defined.

The sample consisted of 160 managers who kept the diary for four weeks, and whose recording had passed several checks for reliability. The managers were volunteers. The sample is therefore not a random one, but it includes, as was planned, middle and senior managers in production, marketing and sales and accounting and some more specialised managers. The managers worked for companies that varied widely both by industry and by number of employees.

2 How the Managers Spent their Time

This book analyses the way in which 160 managers spent their time during four weeks. It looks at similarities and differences in their use of time and tries to find out the reasons for them. This chapter examines working hours, places of work and the time spent on observable activities. It seeks to answer such questions as: How many hours did the managers work? Who worked the longest or shortest hours, and why? How much time did the managers spend in their own offices? Did many of them take work home? How much time did they spend on paperwork, and why did some of the managers in similar posts spend much more time than others?

In this chapter, and in those that follow, the average time that the managers spent on a particular activity is given, as well as the range. It should be remembered that this is the average for the sample of 160 managers. They were a varied group of middle and senior managers, drawn from a great variety of manufacturing companies, but an average for this group is unlikely to be the same as one would get if one could study a representative sample of all middle and senior managers in British manufacturing industry. An analysis of how a different group of managers spent their time would produce a different average for at least some of the activities. Hence the range of variation will often be more important than the average, as the range indicates the extent to which managers may vary in the way that they spend their time. Average figures from other studies are given for comparative purposes.

HOW LONG DID THEY WORK?

The average hours worked by the 160 managers was 42¼ a week. This includes time spent in official entertaining, in company social activities, and in working at home, but it excludes non-working lunches and any other non-working periods in excess of five minutes at a time. Since the latter are not normally excluded when calculating working hours, 43 or 44 hours a week is probably the figure that should be used when making comparisons with other studies. Burns's study of seventy-six managers showed that they worked 41½ hours a week, but his total included fewer sales managers, who tend to work the longest hours.[1] The sixty-six middle managers studied by Horne and Lupton worked an average of 44 hours during the one week that they kept the diary.[2] The figures for these studies are sufficiently close to each other to suggest that they may give a reasonable picture of working hours of a cross-section of middle and senior managers at that time. These hours were shorter than the average hours worked, then, including overtime, by adult males in the UK – though we do not know how much non-working time was included in the official figures.

There are no comparable studies of actual working hours of middle and senior managers in the UK in the 1980s. Since then official working hours have reduced for all levels of staff. Official hours for bank staff, for example, in the autumn of 1986 were 35 hours for all staff including managers, and for most employees in a recent review were under 40 hours.[3] There is now probably a wider diversity of hours worked by middle and senior managers across companies, with top managers in most working longer hours. A comparative study of 400 senior managers in Britain and the USA in 1981 found that both worked a 50-hour week.[4] Average working hours may conceal a wide range of hours as is shown in Figure 2.1.

The average hours worked by the 160 managers ranged from less

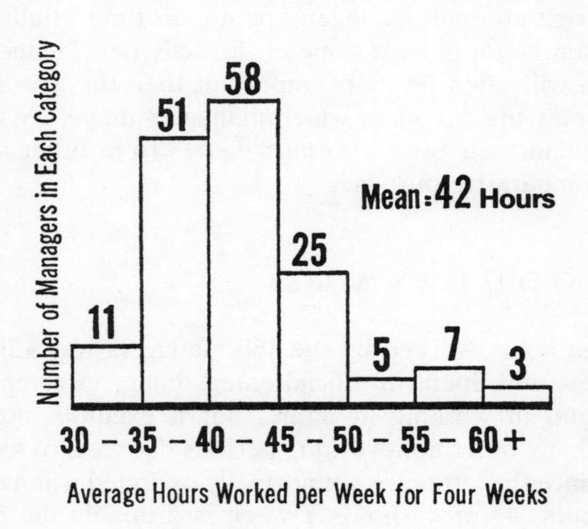

Figure 2.1 Range of average hours worked per week for four weeks

than 35 to over 60 hours a week. This variation seemed to be due more to differences in the type of job, than to differences between companies. Two other studies, however, did find marked differences between companies. These studies may be a better guide to company differences because they had a smaller number of companies in their sample with more managers in each company taking part in the research. Burns, whose seventy-six managers came from eight companies, found that the average hours per week worked by managers in the same company ranged from 37 in one company to 47 in another. Horne and Lupton found a range between companies of 39 to 54 hours per week. Neither study gave figures for differences within companies. Five companies in the present study had five or more managers taking part in the research: the largest number was eleven. In four of the companies the difference between the hours worked by managers in the same company ranged from 12 to 20 hours a week. In only one company did the cooperating managers work similar hours. In this company the seven participating managers worked an average of 37 hours, none of them for more than 39 hours. Even this consistency may have been due to the kind of jobs held by the seven, who did not include any sales or works managers.

In the sample as a whole, the average hours worked by the heads of different functions tended to be longer in some functions than in others. The thirty-four sales managers worked the longest, an average of 44 hours a week. Yet this figure understates the number of hours of many sales managers since it was an average of two groups. Members of one group often left their own offices to visit area sales offices and customers. These managers worked considerably more than 44 hours a week because they spent so much time travelling. Members of the other group worked mainly in their own offices. They had shorter hours. The thirty-six works and production managers averaged 43 hours a week. This was 3 hours longer than the average for the accountants, company secretaries and office managers.

The main cause of long hours was time spent in travelling, which was generally in addition to the normal working hours. Social activities such as company parties and customer entertainment were another cause of longer hours. The three managers who averaged 60 hours or more a week for the four weeks – the highest was 63 hours – were sales managers who averaged 14 hours a week travelling. One of them worked for a company which had four other managers taking part in the research, none of them sales managers, who averaged only 41 hours a week. The twelve managers who averaged 50 to 59 hours a week consisted of three sales managers, four works managers, three area distribution managers, working for the same large company, and two general managers. They spent an average of 9 hours a week travelling.

The eleven managers who worked less than 35 hours a week included three working for the same large company. Two of them were in the secretarial department and the other was the production control superintendent. They worked from 9 till 5, five days a week, with an hour and a half for lunch. The other managers with short hours were three of the sales managers, who were primarily concerned with paperwork, one chief works engineer, several accountants, one company secretary and one office manager. None were works managers. Burns suggested that it was the executives with farly well-defined functions such as accountants and production controllers who worked the shortest hours.[5] This suggestion agrees with the differences found in the working hours of our sample.

Differences between functions and between companies account for part of the variation in working hours. Another factor is the level in the hierarchy. Both Burns and Horne and Lupton found that the more senior the manager, the longer the hours. Burns found that heads of concerns, or their immediate subordinates, worked much longer hours than the other managers. Horne and Lupton found that the average hours worked per week increased an hour or two with each level nearer the chief executive. Reliable comparisons between levels cannot be made for the 160 managers as there is not a large enough number at different levels in the same company. The most reliable comparisons would be between those who were in the same function and in the same company.

WHERE THEY WORKED

The idea of managers as people who spend all their time in their own office or works receives little support from the evidence in the managers' diaries. The average time spent in their own establishment was 75 per cent. The distribution is given in Figure 2.2, which shows that most managers spent a little longer than the average, and that a few spent much less time there.

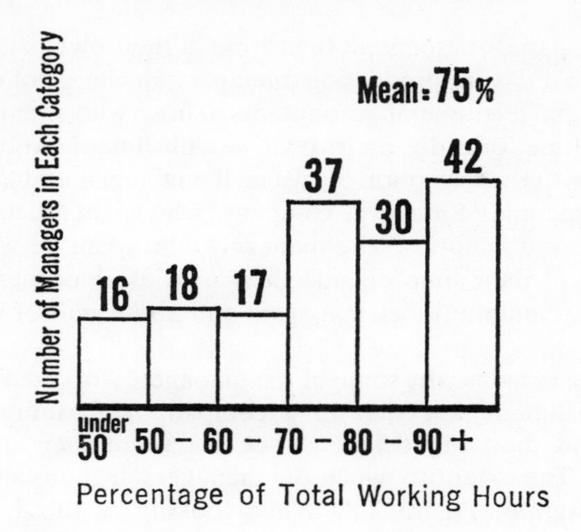

Figure 2.2 Range of time spent in own establishment

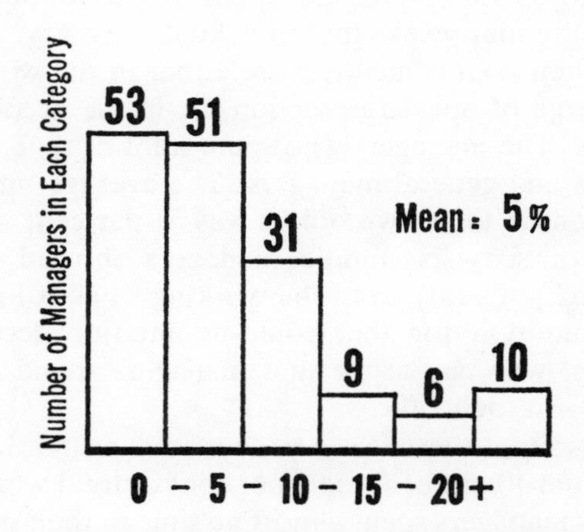

Figure 2.3 Range of time spent visiting other units of the company

Very few managers spent all their time in their own establishment. The few who did were production managers, in charge of one section of a works, and a couple of accountants. Those who spent more than half their time outside their own establishment were all sales managers, with the exception of two civil engineers, and a director of production planning for a large company, who spent much of his time touring different factories. The managers who spent between 30 and 50 per cent of their time outside their own establishment included most of the remaining sales managers and about half of the general managers.

One of the reasons why some of the managers worked outside their own establishment was that in a company with more than one establishment they might have to spend part of their time visiting other units. The extent to which the managers did so is shown in the previous diagram, Figure 2.3. When looking at this it should be remembered that the sample of this study was weighted towards the larger companies where such visits would be more common than in the smaller ones.

The amount of time, excluding travelling, that managers spent working away from their own company is shown in Figure 2.4. The average for the sample was 9 per cent, or about four hours a week. Only twenty-two of the managers spent no time outside their company during the four weeks that they kept the diary. Those who worked only in their own company were either in the works, where they were in charge of one large section, or in the accounting and secretarial offices. The managers who spent a lot of time away were some of the sales and general managers. The average time that the 160 managers spent in their own offices was 51 per cent. Horne and Lupton's study of sixty-six middle managers showed an almost identical figure (52 per cent). Half the working week is long enough to provide ammunition for the would-be interior decorators of managers' offices, who can argue that managers spend more than 1000 hours a year in their offices.

Figure 2.5 shows that there was a wide scatter round the average. The range was from 10 per cent to 90 per cent of total working time. Some of the sales managers spent almost no time in their own offices. Those who spent most time there were mainly accountants. Personal preference obviously had some effect on where people worked; some may have preferred to ask people to come to see them, others may have liked to visit people in their own offices. Figure 2.6 shows that about one in six of the managers spent no time travelling. One in

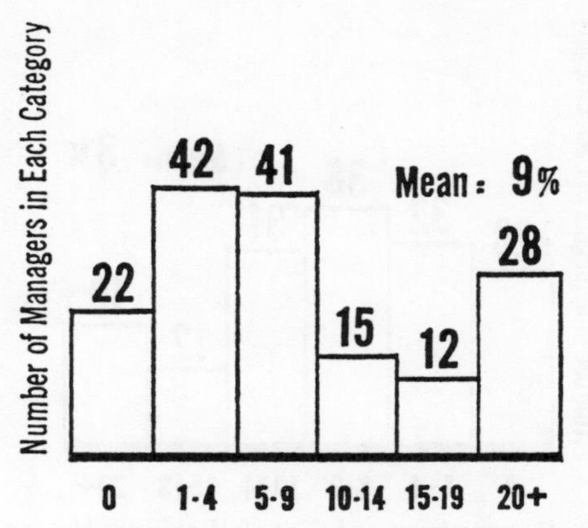

Note: This figure excludes time spent travelling, which is shown in Figure 2.6

Figure 2.4 Range of time spent working outside the company

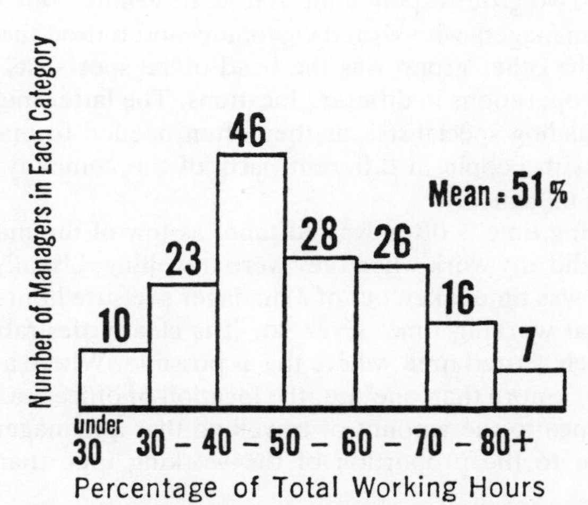

Note: Four area sales managers, working for a large company, are not included in the figures, because they operated from their own home and had no office in the company

Figure 2.5 Range of time spent in own office

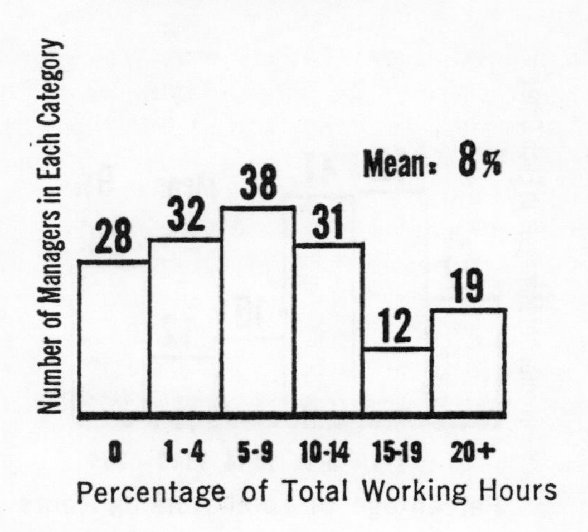

Figure 2.6 Range of time spent travelling

eight spent a fifth or more of his time in travelling. The average was 8 per cent. Two groups spent a lot of time travelling. One of these was the sales managers who visited customers and toured their area sales offices. The other group was the head office specialists who had to advise on operations in different locations. The latter might be called the 'persuading specialists', as they often needed to make personal contacts with people in different parts of the company whom they sought to influence.

Travelling time is often wasted time, as few of the managers said that they did any work when they were travelling. Usually, as we saw earlier, it was time taken out of a manager's leisure hours, not out of the normal working time. Even so, it is clearly desirable to try to reduce such wasted time, where this is possible. Where a company is spread over more than one site, the location of offices can make a lot of difference to the amount of travelling that a manager has to do, and hence to the proportion of the working time that is usefully spent.

Physical layout can influence how managers divide their time between different places of work. Several accountants who were asked about the unusually high proportion of time that they spent in their own offices said that the reason for this was the glass partition between their office and the main office, which enabled them to see and sense what was going on without leaving their desks. This they thought was a good layout. Others were less satisfied with the location of their offices. The chief accountant of one company, employing 200 people, criticised the fact that the offices of all the senior managers in this small company were in a building separate from the factory and general offices, which slightly reduced the frequency of his contact with his staff and considerably reduced the effectiveness of his supervision. This accountant, like those with the glass-partitioned offices, obviously valued the effects of the boss's eye.

Few of the managers took much work home, and almost none did so regularly. If the four area sales managers who worked from home are excluded, the average time spent working at home was about 1½ per cent. The group that did most work at home was the sales managers, probably because they went straight home after a sales trip. Over half the managers did no work at home during the four weeks.

ACTIVITIES

A sea of paper?

Yes for some, no for others. Managers varied enormously in the amount of time they spent on writing, dictating, reading and figurework. The average was 36 per cent of total working time, with a range from 7 to 84 per cent. The average is made up of 26 per cent spent on writing, dictating and reading company material, 8 per cent on figurework – though in some jobs it may have been difficult to separate figurework from writing – and 2 per cent on reading external material for work purposes. The range of time the different managers spent in all forms of paperwork is shown in Figure 2.7.

The accountants, as one might expect, spent most time on paperwork, and especially on figurework. The manager who spent the highest proportion of time, 84 per cent, on paperwork was the chief accountant for a fairly large printing firm. He controlled thirty people, but he had few discussions of more than five minutes either with his colleagues or with his subordinates. Another manager with a very high proportion of time spent on paperwork, 77 per cent, was the head of the budgetary control and standard costs section of a large company. He had few contacts outside his own small section. His paperwork was often done in company with his subordinates. A

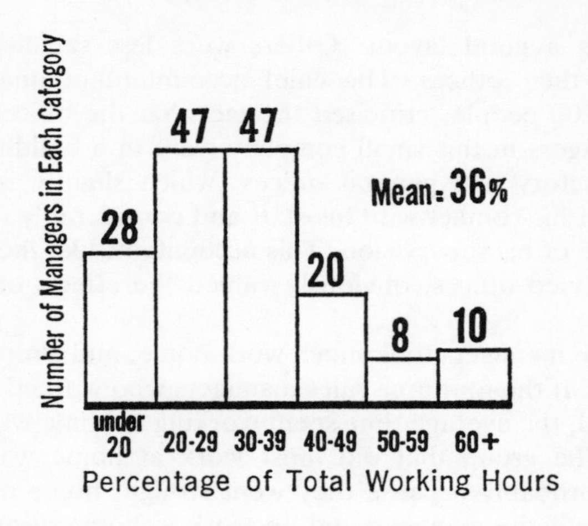

Figure 2.7 Range of time spent on all paperwork

third manager who spent a lot of his time on paperwork was the deputy company secretary of a large company, one of whose duties was to act as secretary to a number of committees.

Many of the accountants spent a lot of time on paperwork, but four spent less than the average amount of time for the whole sample. Three of them played an active part in general management; the fourth ran a large punched-card section, which was more like a production unit. All four worked for large companies. This runs counter to the general belief that the amount of paperwork increases with the size of company. Often it may do so, but so may the need for managers to spend more time in interdepartmental discussions, leaving them with less time for paperwork.

The amount of paperwork is also likely to be affected by the geographical distribution of the company. One of the works managers, who spent 38 per cent of his time on paperwork, said that this was due to the amount of correspondence with the specialist departments at the distant head office of the group of companies to which his works belonged.

The managers who spent exceptionally little time on paperwork included several of the general managers of companies employing under 1000, a few of the works managers and one of the sales managers. Size was not the only explanation. One of the works managers of a large works said he spent most of his time discussing the constant changes that took place in a research and development atmosphere and in trying to prevent them affecting the programme. Burns, it may be remembered, found that the greater the rate of change the more time was spent in discussions, hence the less time left for paperwork.[6] Joan Woodward, in her study of the organisation of 100 firms, found that the amount of paperwork was greatest in assembly-line production firms. It was lowest in companies producing one-offs and small batches, and in process industries.[7]

Young men who think that when they are senior managers they will spend a lot of time dictating to, or talking with, a pretty secretary, will be disillusioned by the record of the 160 managers. We shall see later that most spent little time with their secretaries, even if they had one. As far as can be judged, they also spent little time dictating either to a secretary or to a machine. In this study correspondence and dictating were not recorded separately, as the pilot study had shown that in some jobs it was difficult to distinguish them from other forms of writing and reading. Few of the managers mentioned dealing with their correspondence in the separate record that they filled in of the three activities that had taken most time each day. Works managers, in particular, tended to spend very little time on dictation. As one manager of a large works put it: 'I think that it is typical of production work that a manager does little correspondence or other dictation. I share my secretary with one of my staff. In addition to the normal secretarial jobs she has time for specific work to do with the general administration of the works.' Sales managers spent more time on correspondence, some as much as an hour a day. A few specialist engineering managers, who were responsible for deciding on tenders, spent even longer.

Most of the managers spent very little time on reading work literature that originated outside the company. The average was only 2 per cent. Many read little or nothing. This fact probably upsets few stereotypes of the industrial executive. Seven managers spent much longer than the others, from 10 to 15 per cent of their time on external reading. These were three accountants, two research managers, one general manager, and a head-office engineering chief, who spent part of this reading long tenders. Only the general manager recorded doing any of this reading at home.

Some studies of how managers spend their time have said how long the managers spent 'thinking'. The experience of this study suggests that most managers spent little or no time just thinking. They are more likely to be reading or writing as well. Hence asking them to record 'thinking' as a separate activity may be asking them to make an artificial distinction between thinking and other activities.

The boss's eye

In some jobs it is important for the manager to make a personal inspection to ensure that all is going well. This is most true where the manager, like a works manager or senior nurse, is responsible for a definite physical area. An experienced manager will quickly be able to spot if things are not going well. A personal tour can also have a morale value.

In some jobs there may be little need for inspection; the number of subordinates may be small, or the work may not be amenable to visual inspection. As Figure 2.8 shows, more than half the sample spent little or none of their time in inspection, which was defined as a personal tour of the work-place.

All the accountants and company secretaries, and many of the sales managers, did little or no inspection. At the opposite end of the range, five works managers spent a 25–33 per cent of their time on inspection. These five varied considerably, both in the number of people that they controlled (from 100 to nearly 2000) and in the kind of industries in which they worked. The high proportion of time that they spent on inspection may have been due in part to their

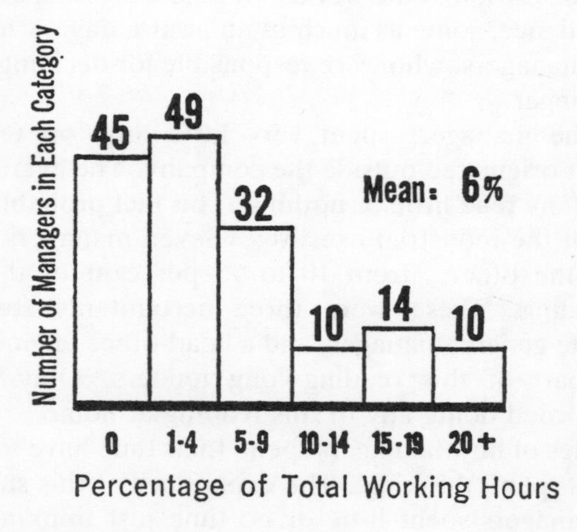

Figure 2.8 Range of time spent in inspection

conception of their job, but clearly it was due also to the kind of job that they had. The five had one thing in common: they were concerned only with running their plant efficiently. They were not involved in the problems of coordinating their work with that of other departments, nor did they play any part in general management. In each of the companies somebody else took the responsibility for coordinating production with other departments. The works manager in the largest works of the five was in charge of nearly 2000 people in a chemical plant. He spent a third of his time on inspection – more than any of the other managers. Another man in the same job might have had a lower figure, as this manager believed in discussing his subordinates' problems with them on the site. He said that he thought that 'managing was like the law – it is not enough for it to be carried out, it must be seen to be carried out. My people, I hope, know that I try to do this by maintaining contacts at all levels.'

How much time the managers spent on paperwork and on inspection seemed to depend upon what else they had to do. Some of those who were asked why they spent so little time on either paperwork or inspection said that it was because they had too many other things to do. This answer may indicate that both are, to some extent, residual activities that are reduced or delegated as the need for discussions with one's colleagues in other departments increases. The works managers who said that they were discussing plans for introducing new plant or developing a new product spent less time on inspection. They may have delegated the task of inspection. The accountants who took part in the general management of the business spent less time on paperwork. It is difficult to know whether this meant that they delegated or streamlined some of the paperwork, or whether there was less paperwork in the company because discussion was often used instead of the written word. The information obtained from this study is not sufficient to show whether either paperwork or inspection really are residual activities, or if they are, whether they are only residual for certain – probably fairly senior – jobs. The idea that some of a manager's activities will be residual does, however, appear plausible, and there seems some evidence to support it from this study. Later research showed that managers have and exercise considerable choice in what they do, which provides another explanation for differences in the time spent on inspection.[8] However, it remains likely that inspection is one of the activities that managers tend to curtail or drop when new tasks arise.

Discussions

Discussions are the dominant activity of nearly all managers, as previous studies have also shown. On average, discussions occupied half the time of the 160 managers. The diary distinguished four types of discussions: informal discussions, which were all those not included under the other headings;[9] committees, defined as prearranged group meetings, which might or might not have an agenda; telephoning; and social activities. The latter included such activities as business lunches, customers' evening entertainment and works socials.

(i) *Informal discussions*

Figure 2.9 shows that informal discussions took nearly half the managers' time. This was, therefore, their major activity. Figure 2.9 also shows how much managers varied in the time they spent in informal discussions. The next chapter, on contacts, will describe some of the reasons for these variations.

(ii) *Committees*

The average time spent in committees was surprisingly small, only 7 per cent, but the range was quite wide, as is shown in Figure 2.10. It seems likely that an analysis of a different group of managers might produce a different average, as the amount of time spent in committees seemed to depend, in part, on company practice.

One in seven of the managers did not attend any committees. At the opposite end of the range, one in fifteen spent a fifth or more of their time in committees. The managers who did not go to any committees were a very mixed group, both in their type of job and in the size of company for which they worked, but they did not include any line managers in large companies. Managers in the works tended to spend more time in committees than those who were in the sales department. Most of the managers who spent a lot of time in committees came from one large company. They are discussed in Chapter 6, on Job Profiles. The manager who had the highest committee attendance was the managing director of a medium-sized company. He attended many external committees, as well as internal ones. This executive is described in a profile in Chapter 6.

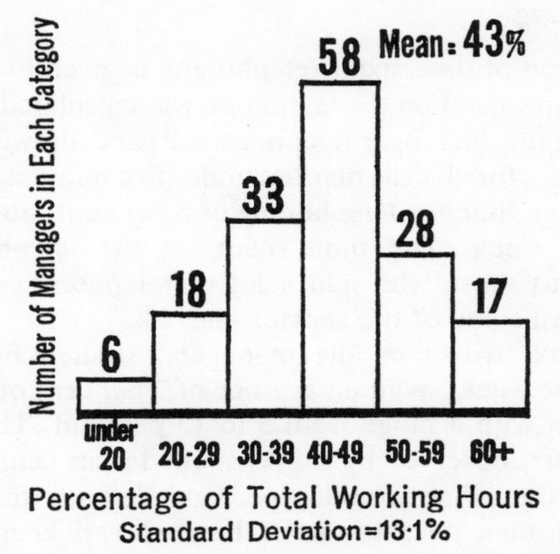

Note: This does not include time spent in conversations during inspection, but does include time spent on the telephone

Figure 2.9 Range of time spent in informal discussions

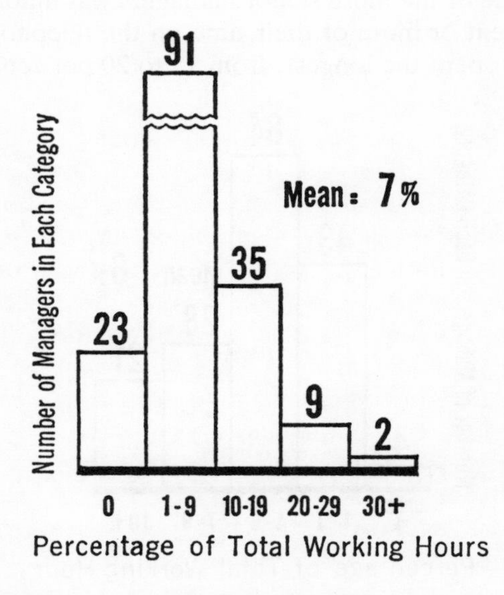

Figure 2.10 Range of time spent in committees

(iii) *Telephoning*

The distribution of time spent telephoning is given in Figure 2.11.

The total time spent on the telephone was calculated by taking the recorded time for the longer telephone calls and allowing an average of three minutes for all calls marked under five minutes. This method gave an average time for telephoning of 6 per cent, about two and a half hours a week. The time spent on the telephone may be understated, as those who had a lot of telephone calls may have failed to record some of the shorter ones.

The sixty-six British middle managers, studied by Horne and Lupton for one week, spent an average of 9 per cent of their time on the telephone, with a range from 5 to 13 per cent. The twenty-five Dutch directors, observed by Luijk, spent 15 per cent of their time on the telephone. One would expect an observer to record more telephone calls than at least some of those who are keeping their own record, but one would not expect such a big difference. The explanation may be a cultural one: Dutch executives may use the telephone when an English executive would prefer a face-to-face talk. The Dutch group were more senior, but there is no evidence from our study that telephoning increased as managers went up the hierarchy. None of the more senior managers was among those who spent 10 per cent or more of their time on the telephone. The four managers who spent the longest, from 15 to 20 per cent, were three

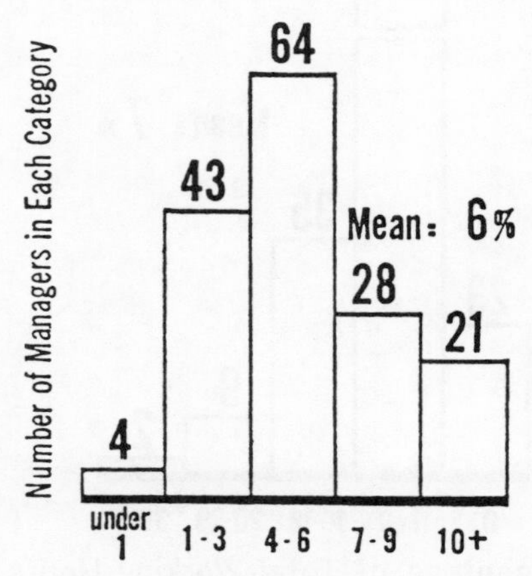

Figure 2.11 Range of time spent telephoning

sales managers and one chief inspector for a motor manufacturer. Most of the others who used the telephone a great deal were works managers.

There may be many reasons why managers spend little time on the telephone. One may be the nature of the job. Another may be the location of the manager's office in relation to those with whom he works. Yet another may be the traditions of the company and of the country in which he works. Then the manager's own preferences will affect how much time he spends on the telephone. Some enjoy the instrument: others feel uncomfortable when using it. The reply of one of the managers, a chief accountant in a medium-sized company, to the question 'Why did you spend so little time (1 per cent) on the telephone?' shows the variety of reasons that may determine whether a manager makes much use of the telephone. He said that his job required him to make few contacts outside the company, so that he rarely had external telephone calls. The company's offices were compact, so that he could easily talk to people in person. He said that he thought that his work was too confidential to be discussed on the telephone. Finally, he said that he preferred to have things in writing. The last reason reflects his own personality, and possibly also the relationships that existed within the company.

(iv) *Social activities*

Managers recorded two main kinds of social activities as part of their working time: one was entertaining customers and other visitors, the other was internal social activities with other managers or with members of their staff. Neither took up much of their time, as Figure 2.12 shows. One-third of the managers spent no time on social activities. The average was 4 per cent, though a diary kept at Christmas time would have produced a higher figure.

The amount of time spent in social activities – which generally meant longer hours – reflected both the kind of company the manager worked for and the kind of job that he held. Some companies had more frequent social functions than others. Sales managers naturally spent most time in entertaining customers. Those with staffs of fifty or more spent longest. Works managers tended to spend more time at works socials than did other managers. Most of the other managers, general managers excepted, usually spent little or no time in social activities. The art of social conversation is not, therefore, one of the things that needs to be taught at management

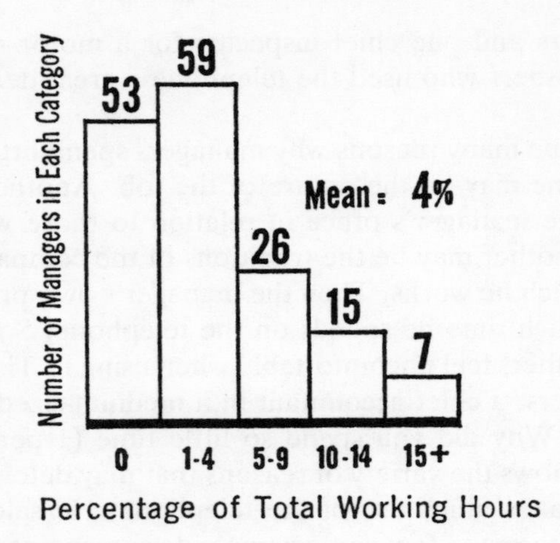

Figure 2.12 Range of time spent in social activities

courses. But if most of the managers spent little time in social conversations – or in business golf – they did spend much of their time with other people. In the next chapter we shall see how this was divided between different categories of people.

SUMMARY

This chapter is the first of four that analyse how the 160 managers spent their time. It discussed how long the managers worked, where they worked, and how their time was divided between activities like inspection, committees and paperwork. It looked at the average times for the 160 managers, at how far some of them differed from the average and at why they did so.

Few of the managers worked very long hours. The average was just over 42 hours a week. The kind of job seemed to be the most important factor in determining how many hours a manager worked. Sales managers tended to work the longest hours – mainly because of the time that they spent travelling – and accountants the shortest hours. Many managers today, particularly senior managers, work longer hours.

Most of the managers spent some of their time outside their own establishment. The average was 25 per cent, though some of the sales managers were away for more than half their time. Two groups spent up to a fifth of their time travelling: the sales managers who visited customers and area sales offices, and the head-office specialists who visited other parts of the company. Half the managers' time, on average, was spent in their own offices, but this ranged from only 10 per cent for a few of the sales managers to up to 90 per cent for some of the accountants. Few of the managers did much work at home, and almost none did so regularly.

Discussions, mainly informal ones, took up more than half the managers' time. Most of the managers could not reasonably complain of the burden of committee attendance. One in seven did not attend any committees and the average was only about half a day a week. Telephoning took almost the same amount of time. Only sales and works managers, and some of the general managers, spent much time in social activities. Even for them these rarely occupied more than two or three hours a week.

Managers who were concerned with problems outside their own department spent more time in discussions and less on paperwork or inspection. It may be that these are, to some extent, residual activities that a manager reduces, or delegates, when he needs to spend more time in discussions with managers in other departments.

3 Other People

This, as well as previous studies, confirms the truth of the statement that 'A manager gets things done through other people'. 'Other people' includes a wide range of contacts, not only subordinates, but also colleagues, superiors, people in other departments, customers and suppliers. This chapter will analyse the time that managers spent with other people. It will start by looking at the amount of time that managers spent by themselves. The remainder of their time will be described as their contact time, that is the proportion of their total working time that they spent talking to other people or listening to them.

HOW MUCH TIME ALONE?

Figure 3.1 gives the amount of time that the managers spent alone.[1] It shows that although on average the managers spent only a third of their time alone, there were wide variations between those at one extreme who had less than 10 per cent of their time alone, to those at the other who had 70 per cent or more.

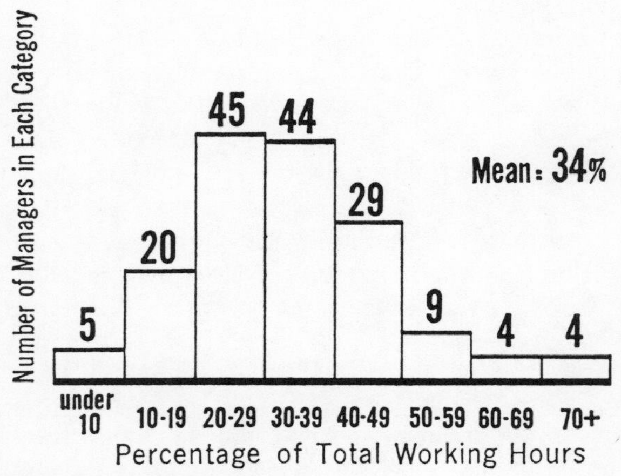

Note: Standard deviation = 14.0 per cent

Figure 3.1 Range of time spent alone

There are jobs that one would expect to involve a relatively large amount of time spent alone. These are the so-called 'back-room jobs', which require a high proportion of specialist and a low proportion of managerial work. Some research managers and specialist engineering jobs are in this category. There are other jobs, such as that of general manager, whose holders are likely to spend little time alone. The fourteen general managers in the sample spent 28 per cent of their time alone compared with an average for the whole sample of 34 per cent, but they had a wide range from 11 to 43 per cent. The two general managers who spent an above average amount of time alone worked for companies employing under 250 people, which, they said, were subject only to a moderate rate of change.

The job of chief inspector is another that one would expect to have a high contact time. Certainly the only chief inspector in the sample, who worked for a motor manufacturer, spent less than 10 per cent of his time alone. He had a wide range of contacts, both inside the company, and with customers, suppliers and others outside. Then there are individual jobs whose special characteristics mean that their occupants are rarely alone. One such was a job that combined the duties of general manager for one division of a company, which employed 350 people, with those of personnel director for the whole company. The manager concerned also spent less than 10 per cent of his time alone.

One would expect certain types of jobs to have a high contact time and others to have a low one. The sample showed differences of this kind, which are discussed in Chapter 6, but it also showed quite large differences between jobs in the same function. The seventeen managers in Figure 3.1 who spent half or more of their time alone included the three research managers, but they also included a few managers from all the other principal functions: works managers, chief accountants, one sales manager and two specialist engineers. Let us try to discover the reasons for these differences between apparently similar jobs.

REASONS FOR THE DIFFERENCES IN CONTACT TIME

Three factors help to determine how much time line managers spend with other people. The first is the extent to which they are concerned with the general management of the business, in addition to the management of their own department. The second factor, which seems to affect at least some of the senior line jobs, is the size of the company or subsidiary for which they work. The third factor whose importance was suggested by Burns is the rate of change. There may be other factors related to the rate of change, such as the nature of the production process or the type of market which also influences how much time a manager will spend with other people. There is some evidence from this study to support the first two explanations. The nature of the sample makes it difficult to examine the third factor and those that may be related to it. There are also other factors which may affect individual jobs, rather than categories of jobs, such as the location of the manager's office in relation to those with whom he or she works.

The first reason for an above average contact time is that the manager is involved in other aspects of the business as well as in the management of a department. This seems to be one of the main explanations for those senior line managers, especially chief accountants, whose contact time is widely different from the average for managers in similar jobs in other companies. We saw in the last chapter that the amount of time that the chief accountant spends on paperwork, which he usually does alone, depends to a large extent on how far he participates in the general management of the company. The contact time of sales and works managers is also affected by the degree to which they take part in general management.

The second factor affecting the amount of time that managers spend with other people is that of size. This factor is related to the first, because the senior accountants, sales managers and works managers in the larger companies tended to spend longer in discussions with managers in other departments. Size comparisons will be made for senior line managers only, as they are the largest group in the sample. Senior managers in production, sales and accounting in companies with more than 1000 employees tended to spend more time with other people than those in smaller companies. This was most clearly marked in the accounting function, possibly because in the larger companies the accountants may have had more to contribute to the general management than in the smaller companies. The five chief accountants who worked for companies with less than 1000 employees, or were chief accountants of a fairly autonomous subsidiary, employing less than 1000, averaged 41 per cent of their time with other people, with a range from 10 to 57 per cent. The seven senior accountants who worked for companies or subsidiaries with more than 1000 employees averaged 74 per cent of their time with other people.[2] The range for six of these accountants was from 73 to 86 per cent. The seventh spent only 49 per cent of his time with other people, but this difference from the six is probably explained by the fact that he was a divisional accountant for a nationalised industry. He was not called upon to spend much time on non-financial aspects of the business, nor did he attend any interdepartmental committees. His contacts were mainly with his subordinates or with his opposite numbers in other divisions. The higher proportion of contact time of the senior accountants in the larger firms was partly due to their spending more time with their immediate subordinates and partly to their spending more time with people in other departments. Each of them had at least three times as many staff as any of the five chief accountants in the smaller firms, though no more immediate subordinates. They averaged 25 per cent of their time with their subordinates, compared with 12 per cent for the accountants in the smaller companies.

There was also some, though a less marked, relationship between the contact time of works managers and the size of their works. The proportion of time that sales managers spent with other people also increased with the size of the company as measured by the number of employees: as with the works managers, these differences are smaller and less consistent than for accountants and may be due to chance.

It is difficult to make meaningful comparisons between the contact time of sales managers in companies of different size when size is measured by the number of employees, because the number of the sales managers' subordinates varies very greatly in companies of the same size. It ranged from twelve in one company employing 2000 to 520 in another company also employing 2000. The first company produced a product that was sold in bulk, the second one that was sold singly or in small batches to companies, and which had to be serviced by the maker. The difference in the size of the two sales managers' staffs is explained, at least in part, by the servicing function of one of them. Yet even when there was no servicing there were considerable differences in the number of the sales managers' subordinates in companies with the same number of employees. A more meaningful size comparison for sales managers may be sales turnover, but unfortunately not all the sales managers gave this information.

The third reason why managers spend a high proportion of their time with other people, according to Burns's study cited earlier, is a rapid rate of change. This may make it necessary for managers to meet frequently to try to sort out the problems arising from change. This study does not lend itself to a comparison between the rapidity of change in the company and the amount of time that managers spend with other people. Managers were asked to say if their companies had a rapid, moderate or a small rate of change, but since most of them said that there was a rapid rate of change – though in some of their industries this was known to be untrue – the manager's own estimate was rarely helpful.

SINGLE AND GROUP DISCUSSIONS

One can distinguish between discussions with one other person and those that are with two or more other people. On average, the managers spent about the same amount of time in each. The range of time spent in each is given in Figures 3.2 and 3.3. These figures show that managers differed more in the proportion of time that they spent in group discussions than they did in the proportion of time taken by single discussions.

Heads of functions in the large companies tended to spend a higher proportion of their time in group discussions than did their

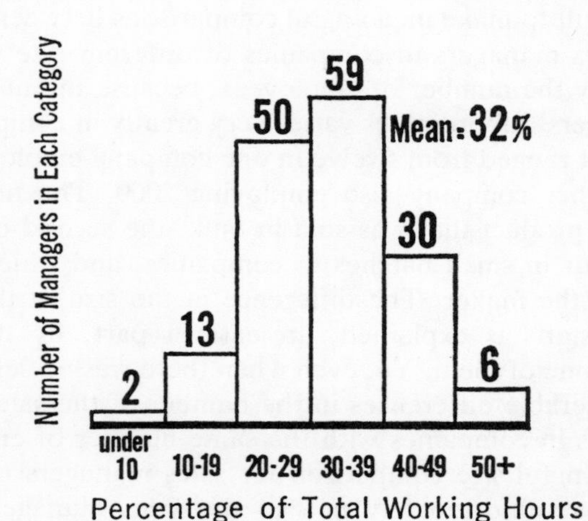

Note: Standard deviation = 9.6 per cent

Figure 3.2 Range of time spent in discussions with one other person

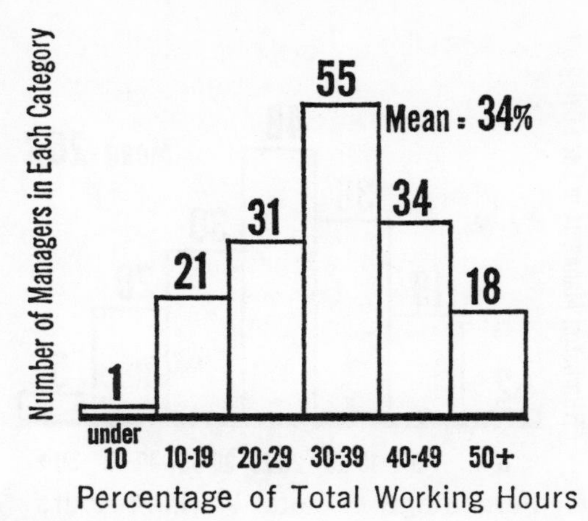

Note: Standard deviation = 12.8 per cent

Figure 3.3 Range of time spent in discussions with two or more people

counterparts in smaller companies, probably because of a greater need for discussions to coordinate the work of the various departments. Another reason for a predominance of group discussions was company practice, since some companies had many more committees and informal discussions than did others of the same size. No doubt, individual differences also played some part according to which type of discussion the manager preferred.

ANALYSIS OF TYPES OF CONTACTS

Internal contacts

(i) *Immediate subordinates*

Immediate subordinates took up more than twice as much of the managers' time on average than any other type of contact. The average time spent with them was 26 per cent. The distribution is given in Figure 3.4. The two managers who had no subordinates are included. They were both specialist engineers working for the same large company, and graded as middle management.

Figure 3.4 does not include the time that managers spent with their secretaries. An average figure for the whole sample would be

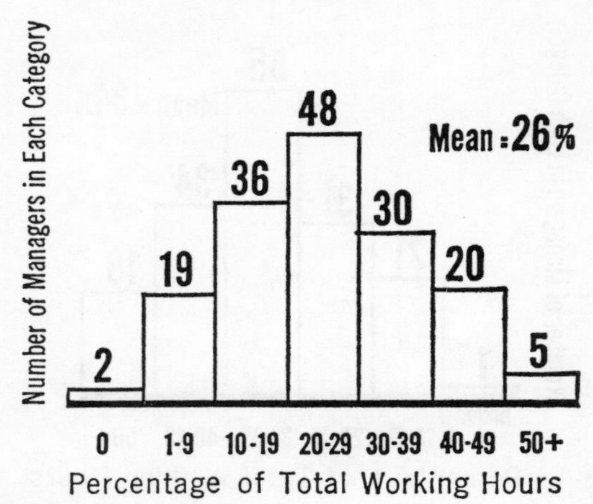

Note: Standard deviation = 13 per cent

Figure 3.4 Range of time spent with immediate subordinates

meaningless as many did not have a personal secretary, and some did not even share a shorthand-typist. The time that managers spent with a secretary or shorthand-typist varied from zero to a quarter of their time. The average was 8 per cent for those managers who had a secretary or shorthand-typist. Works managers tended to spend very little time, and some of the office managers and sales managers a lot of time, with their secretaries.

The managers who spent very little time with their immediate subordinates were mainly managers who provided a specialist service and who had a small staff. Much of their time was spent in discussions with colleagues and with people outside the company. In this category came two of the marketing managers who reported to a sales director, and were not concerned with direct selling. In this group, too, were the specialist engineering managers with very small staffs.

The five managers who spent half or more of their time with their subordinates were four works managers and one factory services manager. One of these, a works manager of a large heavy electrical engineering works, had eleven people reporting directly to him. He attributed his high proportion of time with subordinates to this wide span of control. Another, a factory services manager in a large chemical works, spent most of his time with other people. He had only five people reporting directly to him, and a total staff of 132. He spent little time with his subordinates individually, but one or more of his immediate subordinates attended committees and meetings with him. Managers from this company spent more time at committees and meetings than those in other companies. Another of the five managers, head of a specialised section in the accounting department of a large company, spent nearly half his time with his small group of highly-paid subordinates. He said that this was because he was more a team leader than a manager.

The works managers tended, as one would expect, to spend an above-average amount of time with their subordinates. The 23 works managers averaged 37 per cent of their time with their subordinates, compared with 26 per cent for the sample as a whole. The time spent by the works managers ranged from 12 to 66 per cent. One explanation of this wide variation was size, that is, the proportion of time spent with their immediate subordinates tended to increase with the number of employees controlled by the works manager. Another explanation is some special feature of the job. The works manager who spent least time with his subordinates said that this was because he was also responsible for the buying and selling of a commodity, which meant that many of his contacts were outside the company.

The sales managers tended to spend a below-average amount of time with their subordinates. They accounted for twelve of the fifty-five managers who spent less than 20 per cent of their time with their subordinates. The average for the sales managers was 23 per cent, but the range was also wide, from 14 to 42 per cent. The variations in the amount of time can be explained by two main factors. The first was the size of the company and the number of the sales manager's staff; the second was the extent to which they took part in the general management of the business. The three sales managers who spent least time with their subordinates worked for small companies. The sales managers with the largest staffs, like the works managers, tended to spend longest with their immediate subordinates. A sales manager with a large staff, who worked for a small company, like the sales manager who had a staff of 120 in a company which employed 700, would probably have less help with the recruitment and training of his staff than the sales manager with the same number of staff in a larger company. This would be likely to affect the distribution of his time. The manager just mentioned spent 42 per cent of his time with his immediate subordinates, much of it in recruitment and training. He had a wide span of control – 24 people reported directly to him. Sales managers who spent much of their time with their colleagues discussing other aspects of the business usually had less time to devote to their own staff. The amount of time that managers spend with their subordinates may also vary with the time that they have been in the job. Those who have been in their job some time, and have kept the same subordinates, may well feel that they now need to spend less time with them.

(ii) *Boss*

Figure 3.5 shows the wide range of time spent with the manager's boss.

Only five of the fifteen who reported that they spent no time with their boss – or at least less than 1 per cent of their time – had no boss, as they were *the boss*. The most common reason given for spending little or no time with one's boss was that the manager's boss knew little or nothing about the technical aspects of the job. One manager, for instance, was the only professional engineer in the company. Another reason given for not seeing one's boss was that he was too busy. One works manager said that his boss was in charge of seven factories in the United Kingdom and advised on all production matters in overseas factories. He saw him only four or five times a year. Location obviously affects the time that the manager spends with his or her boss. A boss who is close by can take a much more active interest in subordinates' work – breathe down their necks, if so

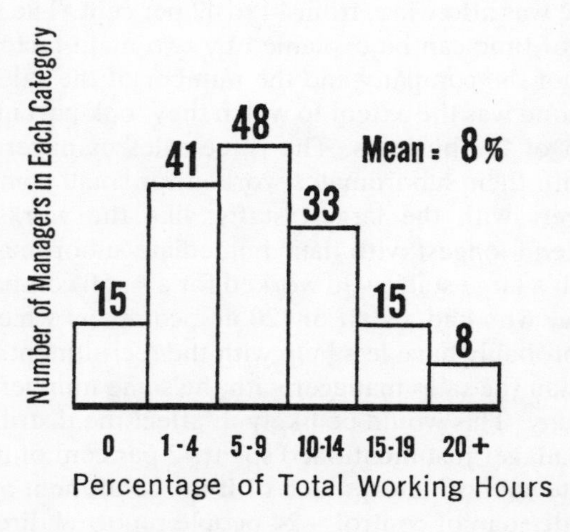

Figure 3.5 Range of time spent with boss

inclined – than one who is in a head office far away.

Eight of the managers spent 20 per cent or more of their time with their boss. Some of them did so because they were discussing an unusual problem. One was a personal manager who had been discussing a threatened strike with the personnel director. Another was sales manager of a company that had just been taken over. A third was a marketing manager who spent part of the month discussing plans for launching a major new product with his boss, the manager director. Managers who had recently taken up a new post generally spent longer with their boss. There were also individual reasons why a manager spent a lot of time with his boss, which arose from the boss's methods of working. One senior manager who spent 18 per cent of his time with his boss said that it was because his boss failed to delegate specific jobs to specific people. Hence two senior people spent time going through an assignment, although a report from one, which was subsequently briefly discussed, would be as satisfactory and save a lot of time. Another manager, a chief accountant, explained that the 21 per cent of his time that he spent with his boss, the managing director, was due to the fact that the latter was often in conference and liked to have his accountant at his side. This was not, however, typical of the relationship between the other managing directors and chief accountants in the sample.

In some organisations and in some jobs the boss is always likely to spend a lot of time with subordinates. Some of the reasons for this can be illustrated by the brewer who attributed the 13 per cent of his time that he spent with his boss to three factors: the fairly high rate of industrial change in their company's breweries leading to frequent consultation with his boss; the seasonal peaks, which lead to a high level of activity and of change in the peak periods, increasing the need to feed new information up and down; the fact that his boss, who was in charge of a number of works, relied on frequent briefing about what was going on.

So far we have discussed how much time the managers spent with people who were in their straight-line hierarchy. Some managers, mainly those in production management, had few other contacts. Some of the managers had a wide range of contacts within the company. Production control managers, works engineers and some managers in the personnel department all tended to spend less time with people in the straight-line hierarchy than most of the managers taking part in the research, and more with other contacts within the company. Three main types of internal contacts, outside the straight-line hierarchy, are discussed below: colleagues, fellow specialists and all others grouped under 'other internal'.

(iii) *Colleagues*

Figure 3.6 shows the distribution of time spent with colleagues, who were defined as those reporting to the same boss. This was the manager's immediate boss, not the professional supervisor. The average was 12 per cent, a little less than half the time spent with subordinates, but more than the 8 per cent with the boss.

Figure 3.6 shows that there was a wide variation in the amount of time spent with colleagues. Five of the managers had no colleagues, as defined. These were the managing directors. Some had colleagues, but rarely needed to see them. This was true of those specialist managers in a large company who operated very much on their own with little need to coordinate the work of their section with that of others. The other main reason why a manager had little or no contact with colleagues was geographical isolation.

There were ten managers who spent 30 per cent or more of their time with their colleagues, the highest figure being 41 per cent. Both the kind of job and the kind of organisation influenced how much time a manager spent with colleagues. Jobs that provide a service for one's colleagues mean close contact with them. This is true of the

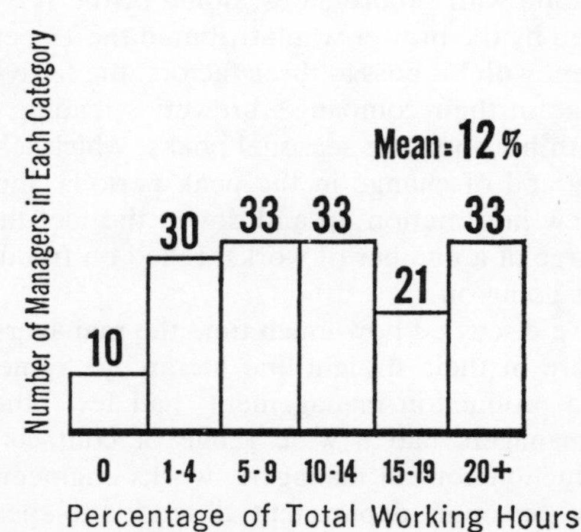

Note: Standard deviation = 9.4 per cent

Figure 3.6 Range of time spent with colleagues

production control managers, who tended to spend a relatively high proportion of their time with their colleagues. It was also true of some senior accountants, who had delegated the management of their department and were primarily concerned with management accounting as an aid to their colleagues. Indeed the time that the chief accountant spends with colleagues may be one indication of his or her contribution to the management of the company.

The needs of the company might require close cooperation between different departments. This was most likely to be true in time of change, when there was more uncertainty and a larger number of overlapping problems to be sorted out. The form of organisation in the company could also influence the amount of time spent with colleagues. In one of the companies a large division was run jointly by four line managers, who therefore had to spend a lot of time in consultation with each other. In another, there was a management advisory committee which had been set up with the aim of encouraging managers to take an interest in problems outside their own departments.

(iv) *Fellow specialists*

Another type of contact, common in large companies, is that between people doing similar jobs elsewhere in the organisation. Figure 3.7 shows the distribution of time spent with fellow specialists, defined as 'those doing a similar job to you in another department, or elsewhere in the parent company'.

Figure 3.7 shows, as one would expect, that many managers spend little or no time with fellow-specialists. The reason for this is that usually there is nobody in that category, due to the small size of the company. The people who spent a lot of time – 30 per cent or more – with people doing jobs similar to their own were works managers of large companies, which had a number of works managers, all of whom might be involved in frequent meetings for coordination and planning.

(v) *Other internal contacts*

Most managers' jobs are limited in their contacts within the company to some or, at most, all of the groups discussed so far, that is: boss, subordinates, colleagues and those doing a similar job, but reporting to a different boss, who were called 'fellow-specialists'. There are a few jobs that bring their holders into contact with other people in the

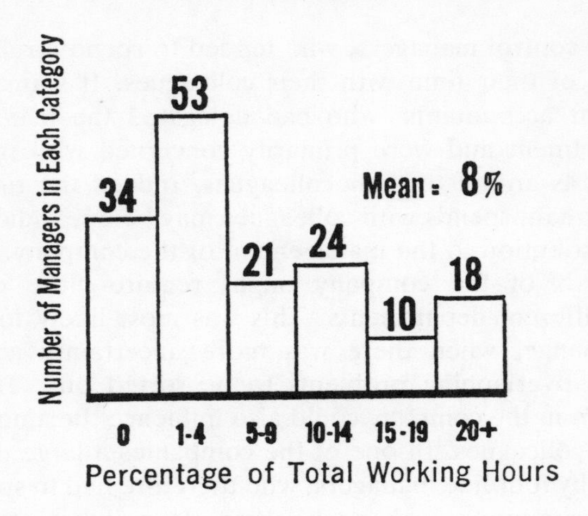

Figure 3.7 Range of time spent with fellow-specialists

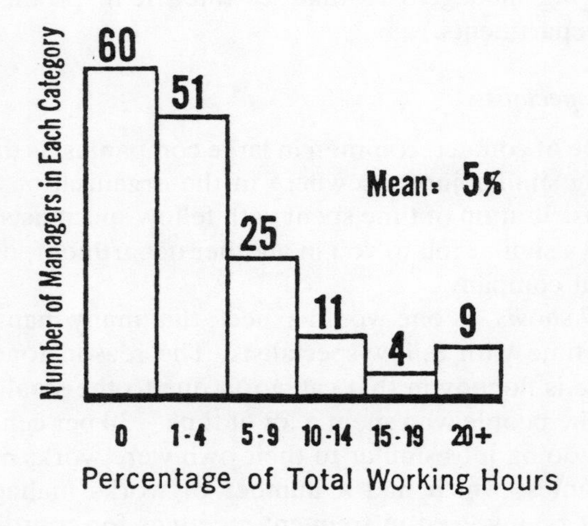

Figure 3.8 Range of time spent with 'other internal' contacts

company. Figure 3.8 shows the distribution of time spent with people in the company who do not fit into any of the categories described so far. These people are called 'other internal contacts'. Figure 3.8 shows that most of the managers spent little or no time with such contacts, but that a few spent quite a lot of time.

The amount of time that the managers spent with 'other internal contacts' was partly a feature of the job and partly a result of the type of organisation. There was probably also some individual variation in the range of contacts. In general, the people who spent most time with 'other internal contacts' were staff engineers whose jobs took them out on investigations in the works. Personnel and training managers also tended to spend quite a large proportion of their contact time in this way, though there are personnel jobs where this is not true, particularly at the policy level in a large company. The influence of the kind of organisation was shown by the fact that those who spent the greatest amount of time with 'other internal contacts' were all working in one large chemical works, where there were a number of cross-level and interdepartmental meetings.

External contacts

External contacts were divided into three groups: customers, suppliers and others. The distribution for customers is given in Figure 3.9 and for 'other external' in Figure 3.10. Contact with suppliers was limited to some of the works managers, to those responsible for purchasing or for the investigation of defects in goods supplied, together with a few of the general managers.

Figure 3.9 shows that about half the managers spent some time with customers. Nearly all the sales managers and some of the marketing specialists did so, as did many of the general managers and some of the works managers. A few of the works managers in the larger works spent as much as 10 per cent of their time with customers.

Figure 3.10 gives the range of time spent with 'other external'. It shows that more than four-fifths of the managers spent some time with external contacts, other than customers or suppliers, and a fifth of them spent 10 per cent or more of their time with them. Some of these external contacts were job applicants. Others included competitors and members of the general public met at trade exhibitions.

Amongst the ten managers who spent 20 per cent or more of their time with people outside the company, other than customers and suppliers, were those whose job was principally concerned with the company's external image. This included the one public relations manager and the one recruitment manager in the sample. It also included those general managers who took part in many activities outside their company, such as committees for their industry and

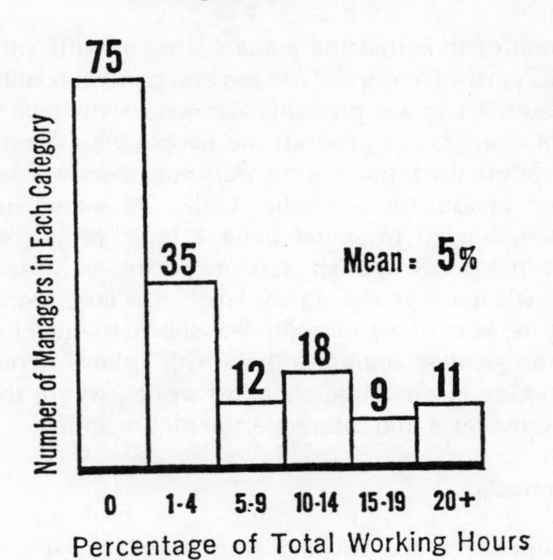

Figure 3.9 Range of time spent with customers

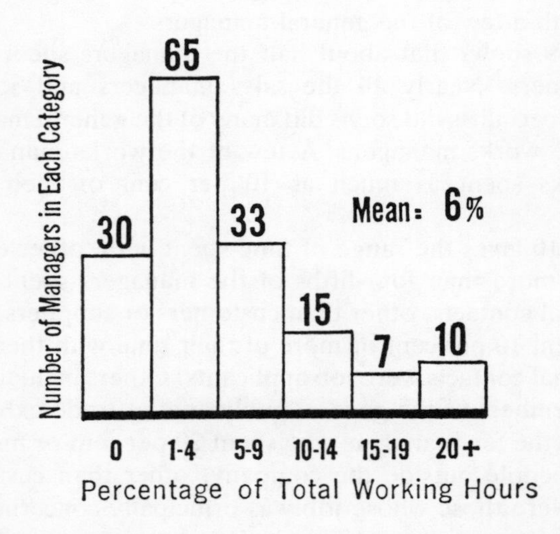

Figure 3.10 Range of time spent with 'other external' contacts

meetings of local management bodies. One man, who was chairman and managing director of his family business, employing 300, and was in this early sixties, spent 35 per cent of his time with people outside his company. He played an active part in his professional body, and was on both local and national committees. He was also chairman of the local Chamber of Commerce and the local branch of the British Institute of Management and was one of the governors of his local university.

The proportion of time that the 160 managers spent with people outside the company is probably higher than it would be in a random sample of middle and senior managers in manufacturing industries. The 160 probably include more managers who take an active part in their professional association, since it was through their professional bodies that many of the managers heard of the research. Managers tended to record work for the professional association as part of their working hours.

RANGE OF CONTACTS

Knowledge of the range of contacts associated with particular jobs in an organisation can be useful in career planning. There are jobs that involve only a narrow range of contacts, which may be limited to one department, to the straight-line hierarchy, or to a small group of colleagues. There are other jobs that bring the holder into touch with a great variety of people in the company – often these are jobs that have a highly specialised subject matter. One example from those cooperating in the research was the standards engineer for a large company. His job involved coordinating the information on which to base a standard. To do this he had to talk to people in many different departments and at many different levels in the company, as well as to suppliers.

There are jobs that are mainly limited to contacts within the company, and those that are primarily oriented outside it. There are jobs that are at the centre of a communications network, where the manager is frequently asked to take action or give information, and where he frequently has to initiate action. A career pattern, like that in the Services, that gives experience both of line management and of staff jobs can provide a good training in the different facets of an organisation. The line jobs provide experience in the exercise of responsibility, but the experience to be gained in some staff jobs should not be underrated. Staff posts often provide a wider range of contacts. Success in them may depend, to a large extent, on the individual's ability to influence and persuade many different kinds of people.

SUMMARY

The 160 managers spent on average two-thirds of their time with other people, but the range was from less than a third for some of the back-room specialists to 90 per cent for the chief inspector and a couple of the sales managers. We saw that the amount of time that a manager spent with other people depended partly upon the type of job. It also depended partly upon how much time the managers spent in discussions with managers from other departments. Those who were only concerned with their own departments tended to spend less time with other people than those who participated in interdepartmental discussions. The size of the company, measured by the number of its employees, also tended to affect the amount of time that the senior line managers spent with other people. The senior line managers in the large companies tended to spend both more time with their immediate subordinates and with their colleagues in other departments. This tendency was most marked amongst the senior accountants.

We distinguished between single and group discussions. On average, the managers spent the same amount of time in each, but they varied more in the amount of time that they spent in group discussions. Managers in large companies tended to spend more time in group discussions than those in small ones, but company practice varied.

Internal contacts were divided into: boss, subordinates, colleagues, fellow specialists and all other internal contacts. Immediate subordinates took up twice as much time on average as any other type of contact. Managers who provided a specialist service, and who had a small staff, spent the least time with their subordinates. Works managers tended to spend the most time. Both the type of job and the organisation of the company affected how much time managers spent with their colleagues (those who reported to the same boss). Some of the most specialised jobs, in terms of their content, had the widest variety of contacts. External contacts were divided into three groups: customers, suppliers and other external. About half the managers had some contact with customers.

Career planning and management development would be helped by a knowledge of the range and the nature of the contacts that are associated with different jobs in the organisation. A line manager could benefit from some experience in staff jobs as these often require different types of contacts, and a different sort of relationship with the people with whom the manager has to work.

4 No Time to Think

One damn thing after another – this is how many managers may feel in one of their 'off' periods. Repeated interruptions and frequent changes of subject matter can give an exhausting sensation of 'o.d.t.a.a.'. Many managers complain that they do not have sufficient time. This may be because they have too much to do. It may be because their job is a highly fragmented one, so that they have few opportunities to catch up with the tasks that require more thought. It may be because they do not organise their work properly. This chapter will discuss the work patterns of different jobs. The term 'work pattern' is used to describe the way in which the day is divided up between long and short activities, the duration of the different activities and the number of interruptions. The last chapter will describe what managers can do to improve the organisation of their work.

Managers' jobs tend to be characterised by the fragmentation of the working day. But just *how* fragmented? This is the first question that this chapter tries to answer. The second is, 'How do jobs compare in the extent and nature of their fragmentation?'

MEASURES OF FRAGMENTATION

The diary provides three possible measures of the amount of fragmentation of a job: one, the number of periods spent alone that are long enough to provide time for the manager to concentrate on a problem; two, the number of fleeting contacts, that is, conversations of under five minutes, either by telephone or face to face; and three, the number of diary entries. Several of the managers who had a very large number of fleeting contacts said they were unable to record them all. This means that their working day was more fragmented than the number of recorded fleeting contacts would suggest. However, this is unlikely to affect the broad comparisons between managers with a large, medium or small number of fleeting contacts, since these managers will still belong to the group with the highest number. The three measures of fragmentation by themselves do not tell us how much of it is inherent in the job, and how much is the result of bad work organisation. We can get some indication of this by looking at the extent to which certain types of jobs have a common fragmentation pattern. We can ask why one manager differs noticeably from others in similar jobs. In many jobs it is possible by good planning to reduce the amount of fragmentation. How this may be done is discussed in Chapter 9.

Number of periods of half an hour or more alone

One measure of a manager's time to think and plan is the amount and length of time that she has to herself. We saw earlier that the sample spent an average of one-third of their time alone, and that only seventeen members spent more than half their time alone. If these periods alone are to be useful for sustained work they probably need to be at least half an hour in length. How often did the managers have this length of time to themselves? Figure 4.1(a) shows the number of periods of this length that they had during the four weeks, but which were interrupted by fleeting contacts. Figure 4.1(b) shows the number they had without interruptions. Both figures exclude time spent travelling alone, as very few managers recorded doing any work while they were travelling. It should be noted that Figure 4.1(b) has been divided into periods of 5 per cent and Figure 4.1(a) into intervals of 10 per cent because of the much smaller number of periods without fleeting contacts.

The figures show that managers had on average just over twice as many periods alone with fleeting contacts as they had without them. However, the interpretation of the former must allow for the fact that they include long periods of time alone, broken only by one or two brief contacts, as well as periods alone that consist only of a succession of telephone calls. Managers averaged roughly one period a day alone of half an hour or longer, with fleeting contacts, and about one period every other day without.

The managers who had very few periods alone of half an hour or longer, either with or without fleeting contacts, included most of the works engineers and production controllers. They also included six managers who spent less than a fifth of their time alone, and therefore might be expected to have few periods of any length alone. There were also two managers whose shortage of periods of half an hour or longer alone may have been due, at least in part, to the way they organised their job, as there seemed to be no clear reason why they should have so exceptionally few. One was the sales manager for a small company producing one-off capital equipment for customers'

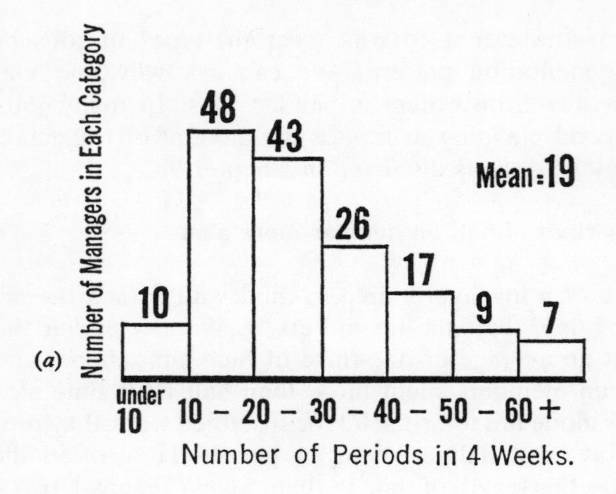

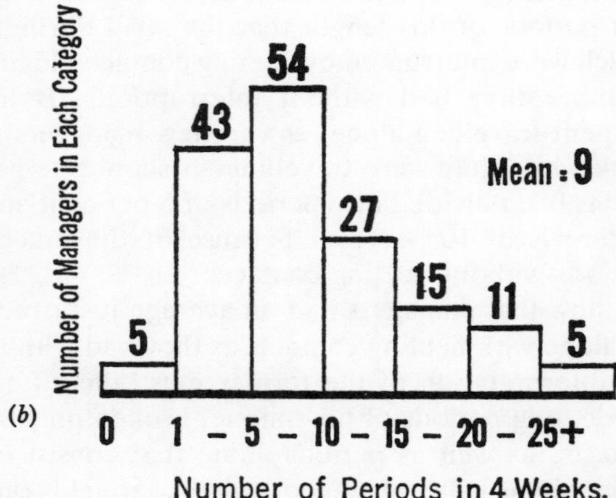

Figure 4.1 (*a*) Number of periods of half an hour or longer alone during the four weeks, broken by brief contacts
(*b*) Number of periods of half an hour or longer alone during the four weeks, without interruptions

individual requirements. He had a relatively large sales forces, which was also responsible for servicing. The other was an engineer who, at the time when he kept the diary, was investigating difficulties in newly commissioned plant. He said that keeping the diary had shown him that he should delegate more detailed work.

Those who had many periods of half an hour or longer alone fell into two groups. The first, those who had a large number of periods alone both with and without fleeting contacts; and the second group, a smaller number, who had a very large number (fifty or more), periods with interruptions but few (under ten) such periods without interruptions. The second group consisted of people who spent more than half their time alone, so though they were bound to have quite a large number of longish periods alone, these were fairly frequently interrupted by fleeting contacts. In this group came a number of accountants, including the accountant referred to in the last chapter, who, although he spent 90 per cent of his time alone, had only seven periods of half an hour or longer alone without fleeting contacts, though he had 61 such periods alone with fleeting contacts. He had an unusually large number of fleeting contacts, an average of thirty-one a day, twenty of them with his subordinates. The other managers who had considerably more than the average of periods of half an hour or more alone, included most of those with a relatively high proportion of time spent alone, as well as some others, such as the area sales managers who worked from home.

Managers who are at the centre of a communications network are bound to have fewer periods alone than those whose work is mainly long-term, and whose information is only called for at infrequent intervals. Yet the considerable variations in the number of periods that managers had alone, which lasted half an hour or more, cannot be fully explained by differences in the type of job. It was also due – more than any other aspect of the work that we considered – to the way in which the individual organised his work.

Number of fleeting contacts

The second measure of the amount of fragmentation of the working day is the number of fleeting contacts of under five minutes; that is, brief conversations either by telephone or face to face. This is related to the first measure, as it is likely to affect the number of periods of half an hour or longer that a manager has undisturbed. Figure 4.2 shows the distribution of the number of fleeting contacts per day. The average was 12, but over half the managers recorded between three and ten a day. The high average is explained by the smaller number of managers who recorded considerably more than 12 a day.

To what extent is the number of fleeting contacts a reflection of the kind of job and to what extent is it a result of the way in which

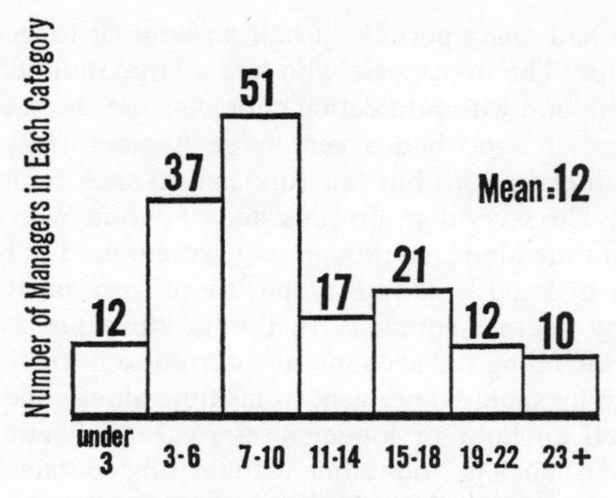

Note: Standard deviation = 7.7

Figure 4.2 Distribution of number of fleeting contacts during the day

managers organise, or fails to organise, their work? The information provided by the diary cannot give us an exact answer to this question, but it can show in which jobs there are a large number of fleeting contacts and in which there are a small number.

The managers who had a very small number of fleeting contacts, under three a day, included some of the sales managers, especially those whose opportunities for fleeting contacts were reduced by their frequent absences from their office, and by the geographical separation of many of their subordinates. Those with a very small number of fleeting contacts also included some of the specialists who had few or no staff. One of these was a back-room engineer, with only one subordinate, whose responsibility was to examine the technical and economic merits of new engineering schemes. Another was a senior accountant in a large company, who was primarily concerned with accounting systems and not directly in control of staff.

Most of the managers with a large number of fleeting contacts were works managers. Some of these contacts would have taken place during their tours of inspection, but this only accounts for a quarter or less. When we look at who the fleeting contacts were with, we find that their subordinates accounted for more than half, and their bosses for very few, usually less than one a day. One of the works managers, who had an average of twenty-one fleeting contacts a day, differed noticeably from the other works' managers who had a large number of fleeting contacts, as only 20 per cent of his were interruptions compared with 50 per cent to 80 per cent for the other managers. He attributed this to the fact that both his door and his telephone were guarded by a secretary who managed to insulate him from inessential interruptions.

The number of fleeting contacts of production managers, and of general managers who were involved in production, seemed to be related to the frequency of short-term changes in the production process. This can be illustrated by the comments of two managers, one with a very small and the other with a large number of fleeting contacts. One, the general manager of a medium-sized subsidiary, who had less than three fleeting contacts a day, attributed this to the fact that his firm produced a rather heavy engineering product which takes a long time to make. He thought that this made for a slower tempo with little need for brief queries. At the opposite extreme was a brewer, in charge of a brewery with 100 employees, who had an average of forty-six fleeting contacts a day. Only about a fifth of these took place during his tours of inspection. He attributed this very large number of fleeting contacts to four factors. One was the seasonal nature of the production. The diary was kept during the summer, the peak output period. He was sure that a smaller number of fleeting contacts would be noted in late autumn and early winter. During the summer, production is under high pressure and changes, both major and minor, occur hourly. Fleeting contacts increase as more new information is passed upwards and downwards. The number of fleeting contacts is also raised by the fact that production planning rests mainly with the production managers, that is, the brewers. The second reason that he gave for the high number of fleeting contacts was that the supervisors often had to check with a superior before reaching a decision on a technical problem. He said that 'Whilst we try to delegate maximum authority, we find, probably more than most industries, that management by exception, as we practise it, leads to a very high number of fleeting contacts.' The third reason that he suggested was the need for quick communication in their type of process industry. The last reason was the location of his office at the hub of the brewery, which made personal contact easy. There was only one brewer in the sample, so no comparisons can be made for individual differences, but although one would expect individual variations, one might also expect that all brewers would record a large number of fleeting contacts in the summer.

Number of diary entries

The third indication provided by the diary of the amount of fragmentation of the working day was the number of diary entries. It should be remembered that these were for recordings of five minutes or longer. The number of fleeting contacts of under five minutes was recorded separately. Figure 25 shows that the number of diary entries per day did not vary as much as the number of fleeting contacts.

The managers who had a small number of entries per day tended to be those who had long periods alone, though they did not necessarily have an above-average amount of time by themselves. Their time with other people tended to be spent at lengthy meetings. They were able to plan their work and to spend long periods on one particular problem, though quite often they might be interrupted by fleeting contacts. The thirteen managers who had the largest number of entries ranged from twenty to twenty-nine entries a day compared with an average of thirteen entries. As most of them also had high scores on the other two measures of fragmentation of the working day, they have already been mentioned.

We have looked at three measures of the fragmentation of the working day. Another possible measure which was considered at the

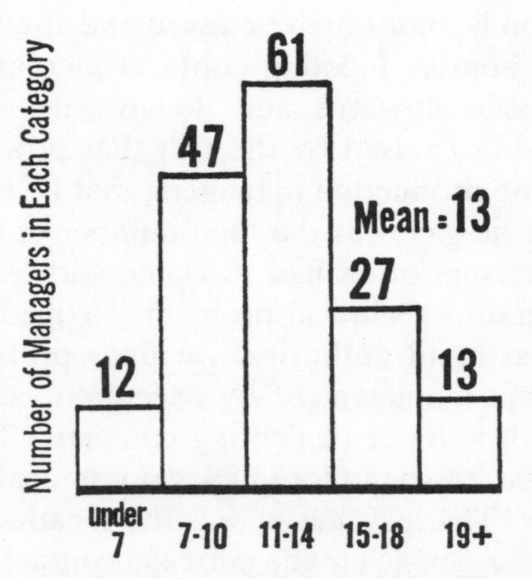

Note: Standard deviation = 4.6

Figure 4.3 Distribution of number of diary entries per day

pilot stage is the number of subjects dealt with during the day. No attempt was made to record this in the main research, because of the difficulty of defining 'subject' unambiguously. One other guide to the amount of fragmentation was provided by each manager's daily description of the activities that had taken most time that day, and how long he had spent on them. Some managers frequently described activities that lasted several hours; others rarely mentioned anything, apart from the occasional committee, that lasted as long as an hour.

PROFILES OF A FRAGMENTED AND AN UNFRAGMENTED JOB

Let us now take a close look at two jobs, one that illustrates a very fragmented job and one a very unfragmented job. The brewer is a good example of a very fragmented job, at least in the peak summer period, but as we have already discussed him at some length, let us take a different illustration.

Mr Arthur was the works manager of a large works in the textile industry.[1] He had twenty-five immediate subordinates and reported to the works director. He made twenty-one diary entries a day, plus twenty-three fleeting contacts, thirteen of which were telephone calls. He worked an average of 7¾ hours a day, so that he averaged about 3 diary entries and three fleeting contacts an hour. During the four weeks he had periods of half an hour or more alone, but only two of these were free from fleeting contacts.

Mr Arthur said that his major decisions concerned production control and balance, and new plant and techniques. He also took part in sales planning, packing planning, plant and machinery purchase and installations, personnel and quality control. The day-to-day coordination of the large number of often highly technical processes took up most time.

Mr Arthur's highly fragmented work pattern can be explained by a number of different factors. One is his job as a works manager. Most of the works managers' diaries showed an above-average amount of fragmentation, as judged by the three measures discussed in this chapter. Another factor, and probably the most important, is the very varied and highly technical character of the production in his factory, which increased the number of problems that he was asked to deal with. Mr Arthur said that his works was an example of a vertically integrated plant, covering all stages of production, from the processing of raw materials to the final product. Mass, batch and process production took place in a highly integrated complex of production divisions. It was, he said, like running several factories under one roof. Yet another reason for his fragmented work pattern is his large span of control. A final reason is the active part he played in general management, which brought him into contact with many people outside his own department. Another person in Mr Arthur's job would be unlikely to have an identical work pattern, but would probably also have a highly fragmented one.

It would be easy to illustrate a very unfragmented work pattern by taking a back-room job that involved a lot of solitary work, but it is more interesting to take one that is similar to the majority of other management jobs in the amount of time spent with other people. Mr Brook was the deputy company secretary of a large company. He was secretary to the top management committee and acted as staff officer to the managing director, when necessary. He had three people reporting directly to him and a total staff of nine. He worked at the London head office, which contained only head office staff.

Mr Brook averaged 3½ diary entries a day and 9 fleeting contacts a day. He worked seven hours a day, so that he made one diary entry approximately every two hours, and had one fleeting contact, usually a query from his secretary, about once every fifty minutes. He spent little time on the telephone: his calls were usually short. Like Mr Arthur, he spent about three-quarters of his time in contact with other people, but much more of it in single conversations. When he was alone it was for lengthy periods of an hour or more.

Mr Brook spent much of his time preparing for the weekly top management committee and for an *ad hoc* committee on organisation. He wrote papers, compiled the minutes and attended these meetings. His other major activity, when he was keeping the diary, was preparing an organisation and instruction manual. He spent the rest of his time on other secretarial matters and correspondence.

Mr Brook's was primarily an administrative and staff job, with few, if any, crises. This is likely to be the main reason for the unfragmented work pattern, but personal style of working also affects the amount of fragmentation. Some of the 160 managers spent much longer working by themselves and had far fewer fleeting contacts. These included some of the managers in charge of specialist services, such as market research.

SUMMARY

This chapter attempted a new type of analysis of managers' jobs by trying to measure the amount of fragmentation of the working day. The phrase 'work pattern' was used to describe the frequency with which a manager's activities and contacts vary. The chapter was written in the belief that the work pattern of a job is one of its distinctive features, which should be taken into account in selection and in planning training needs. We shall see more of the importance of work patterns in the chapter on 'Job Profiles'.

This chapter sought to answer two questions. The first was 'How fragmented were the manager's jobs?' The second, 'How did the jobs compare in the extent and nature of their fragmentation?' Three measures were used to assess the amount of fragmentation. The first was the number of periods alone that lasted half an hour or longer. The second was the number of fleeting contacts, both telephone calls and personal, of under five minutes. The third was the number of diary entries. Managers had on average one period of half an hour or longer alone each day broken by fleeting contacts, and one such period every other day that was undisturbed. The managers who had the fewest periods of that length alone were the works engineers and production controllers. Amongst those with the largest number were some of the accountants. The average number of fleeting contacts recorded per day was twelve. Works managers had the most; and specialist managers, with few or no staff, and some of the sales managers had the least.

The differences between a job with a very fragmented work pattern and one with a very unfragmented one were illustrated by two job profiles. It was argued that although different individuals in the same job will not have identical work patterns, they will tend to be similar, since many, though perhaps not all, jobs have characteristic work patterns. This does not mean that managers can do nothing to modify the work pattern, but that in many jobs they will be unable to change it radically. What a manager may be able to do to limit the amount of fragmentation of the working day is discussed in the last chapter.

5 Variety within Jobs

'Variety is the spice of life.' But what is variety? What is a varied job? Clearly a man who performs an identical action upon identical products on a moving belt has no variety in his job, unless the belt breaks down or the product changes. The manual worker on an assembly line not only does the same thing; he does it in the same place and in contact with the same people. No manager's job is like that. Her place of work will probably change, if only from one office to another. Her contacts are likely to vary. The activities that she performs will change, and not in a set way. She may be dictating at 9 a.m., inspecting the factory at 10 a.m. and be in conference at 11 a.m. Nor is the sequence of activities likely to be always the same. The content, too, will change. She is unlikely to be dictating the same letter or having the same discussion as she had the day before. The time span of the subjects that she is dealing with will also change. In the morning she may decide how to deal with a customer's complaint and in the afternoon continue a discussion on how to launch a new product in six months' time. Later that day she may join a committee that is considering the possible implications of new products that are still at the research stage. This description gives some idea of the different ways in which managers' jobs may be varied. Let us look at these in more detail.

DIFFERENT KINDS OF VARIETY

Place

In most jobs one's place of work is restricted. The postman has a definite round, the typist a desk and chair – the number of square feet per office worker is laid down. The surgeon has more variety. He moves between the out-patient depatment, his consulting room, the operating theatre, the wards, and he may go to patients' homes. The accountant's place of work is likely to be more limited than that of the surgeon. He will spend most of his time in his own office, some time in the rest of the accounts department, in his boss's office and perhaps in a conference room. His work is unlikely to take him outside his own establishment, or even outside the offices. He need spend none of his time travelling. His is correctly described as an office or desk job, but top financial jobs offer more variety.

The accountant's job is bounded by the office walls; most production jobs are confined within the factory gates. Promotion on the works side generally brings with it greater mobility; the works manager and the chief engineer will join in discussions with their office colleagues. They may go to other works in this country and possibly abroad to look at new equipment and new methods. The works manager may visit important customers. Production jobs are likely to provide greater variety in the place of work than those in finance. The place of work is also likely to be less predictable. It is managers in the works who need to carry bleeps, not those in finance or administration.

Most hard to find will be the sales manager, whose place of work is often least predictable. Some sales managers may be nearly as office-bound as their financial and administrative colleagues, but others will do much of their work outside the company. One week may bear little resemblance to the next. A sales manager may spend one week away from the company, and the next catching up on paperwork in the office. Some, even in very large companies, have no office, but work from home.

The managers with the greatest variety in their place of work are some of the staff specialists in large companies. They go where they hope their advice will be useful and live in other people's offices. The more widely spread the company's works, the more mobile they must be. The need to keep abreast of developments in their speciality will also take them to other companies, to research institutions, and to professional conferences at home and abroad.

People

Managers' contacts can be varied in different ways. They may see very few people or a large number. They may see only those in their own department, or may meet people in other departments as well. They may work mainly with immediate colleagues, or may have discussions with people at many levels in the organisation. Their contacts may be confined to their own company or they may have many contacts outside. Many managers may see no one but their boss, their subordinates and their immediate colleagues. Their variety of contacts may be limited in all ways, by number, by levels and by department. Others, like the works manager who was in charge of one works employing 1600, part of a large company, have many more contacts. He saw his boss, the production manager of a product division, every one or two weeks. He spent a lot of time with his immediate subordinates and knew many of the workers whom he saw on his inspection tours. He joined in weekly discussions with his colleagues from other works. He also had contact with people from sales, finance, engineering and research. His contacts were extensive. They ranged vertically in production from the bottom to nearly the top of the company, and horizontally to include all other departments. But although he worked for a large company he almost never saw anyone outside his own company. In this he may be rather unusual, as many of the works managers saw customers and suppliers and some also had professional contacts. We saw in the chapter on 'Other People' that some of the head office specialists also had company-wide contacts.

A different kind of variety of contacts can be illustrated by one of the sales managers who worked for a company which employed 500 people. He frequently saw his small sales staff, both those on the road and in the office. He discussed production and delivery problems with the works manager. He saw the managing director several times a week. So his contacts inside the company were quite wide but did not include the manual workers or the office staff outside the sales department. Much of his time was spent outside the company, visiting important customers and in travelling. His contacts varied greatly from week to week, depending on whether or not he spent the week in the company.

Content of work

The content of a job may be varied either in depth or breadth or, though this is not as usual, in both. A specialist post may provide considerable variety within its own speciality, particularly if the subject is developing rapidly. A general manager's job, or that of any senior line manager who takes part in the general management of the company, provides variety in breadth, that is, in the range of problems.

There are two main factors that help to determine how much variety there is in the content of a job: one is its position in the hierarchy and the other is the amount of change affecting both the company in general and that function in particular. In junior management jobs short-term decisions are likely to predominate.

More senior managers will be concerned with much longer-term, more varied decisions, where the element of uncertainty is much greater. The process of decision-making may also be spread over a long, discontinuous period. Another factor that will increase the amount of variety in a job is participation in discussions of problems outside the manager's own department.

TWO WORKS MANAGERS COMPARED

Two of the works managers who took part in the research can illustrate the differences in the variety of jobs. Their jobs were similar in many respects in their function, level and number of subordinates. Yet one job was much more varied than the other. Mr Turner was the works manager for a company employing 370 people in a small provincial town, which made one-off precision engineering equipment. He had 267 subordinates. Mr Salter was works manager for two near-by factories in London, which together employed 350. They were part of a medium-sized company that became a subsidiary of a large company a few years ago. One factory made a wide range of products in batches. The other operated a continuous process. Mr Salter reported to the deputy managing director of his subsidiary company, Mr Turner to the managing director. Both men were about the same age. Neither had a degree, but both had attended a number of management courses.

Mr Turner said that he was responsible for the efficient running of the works, based on the sales budgeted figures, for all production, personnel, costs, buying, inspection, also application tests, for building of special-purpose machines from the receipt of the customer's order to the packing and despatch from the warehouse, and for all maintenance work both at the works and at the head office a mile away.

Most of his time was spent dealing with production and trying to ensure that the subcontract items arrived at the dates promised. His periodic and occasional duties included the preparation of labour and cost details. His main decisions concerned the modification of machines for more efficient operation, the continual redeployment of labour and the placing of subcontract orders.

Mr Turner spent a high proportion of his time, 85 per cent, with other people, divided about equally between single and group discussions. Most of his contact time was spent with the seven people reporting directly to him. His conversations with the rest of his staff rarely exceeded five minutes at a time. His boss, the managing director, took up 11 per cent of his time and his colleagues only 5 per cent. Suppliers, who were his main external contacts accounted for a fair amount of time each week, an average of 12 per cent. He interviewed all suppliers and kept in close touch with them. During the month he visited a supplier's works on a Sunday to discuss the production of components. He occasionally saw customers who came for demonstrations. His only contact with the general public was with parties of school-leavers and apprentices on visits to the works.

His daily work pattern varied. He started work about 8.15, usually working on his own; this and the end of the day were his two main opportunities to work alone. Most of this time was spent preparing production and cost statistics. Correspondence took up little of his time. He had no regular period for dictating and did not dictate every day. He did a tour of inspection almost daily, but not at a set time. By 9 a.m. or shortly afterwards he would be in discussions for nearly all the rest of the day, most of which were held in his own office. He always started his afternoon work at 1.30 and broke for lunch between 12.30 and 1 p.m. He stopped work usually at 6.30. He worked longer hours than most of the managers who took part in the research, an average of 55 hours a week, with a range from 50 to 68. The works operated seven days a week. He was always there on Saturday morning and usually for a few hours on Sunday.

His discussions were usually lengthy but were frequently interrupted by fleeting contacts. Nearly all the discussions concerned his own department and were usually about immediate production or purchasing problems. Personnel problems, at least during the month that he kept the diary, took up very little of his time. He attended two weekly committees, one a works production committee on Monday afternoon, the other on Tuesday afternoon, an interdepartmental committee to discuss incoming orders.

There was little variation in his weekly figures during the four weeks that he kept the diary. The greatest range was from 41 per cent in the lowest week to 60 per cent in the highest week, in the proportion of time that he spent with his immediate subordinates. Mr Turner's job is an example of a non-cyclical job that provides a certain amount of variety but within a fairly limited range of problems. The production of specialised engineering equipment and the contact with suppliers provides more variety than that enjoyed by a manager of a works producing a standard product. Yet the variety is less than in a works where there is more rapid technical change. Many of his problems had a similar content, such as how to get suppliers to deliver on time, and how to redeploy the workers. Most of his work was limited to production. He had little contact with his colleagues, apart from one weekly meeting on incoming orders. He played little part in the general management of the company, though during the month he was asked to attend a board meeting where there was a general discussion on the expansion of the company and on the type of building and labour required for increased production.

Mr Salter worked shorter hours than Mr Turner, an average of 44, but then he did not go in at the week-end, though one factory was on continuous shift. A manager of a London works is much less likely to visit the factory at the week-end than the manager of a factory in a small provincial town who may live close by.

Mr Salter started work shortly after 8.30. His lunch was variable, sometimes a short break for a snack, sometimes an hour, sometimes a longer business lunch. He stopped work between 5 p.m. and 5.30. He had more time to himself than Mr Turner – about a third of his working time was spent alone – though some of this was working at home. He usually spent the morning in a variety of fairly short discussions, with one or more of his seven immediate subordinates, but sometimes he had ten to twenty minutes working on his own. He spent less than 33 per cent of his time with his subordinates, compared with Mr Turner's 53 per cent. Much more of his time was spent in talking with his colleagues, 20 per cent compared with Mr Turner's 5 per cent. He attended more committees than Mr Turner, but they met less frequently. Correspondence also took up little of his time. He dictated for short periods two or three times a week but not at any set time.

The afternoon also followed no pattern. Like the morning, most of it was usually spent in discussions interspersed by short periods of working alone. On most days few of his discussions lasted as long as half an hour. His longest activities were occasional inspections carried out with other people, though in total he only spent 3 per cent of his time on inspection. Committees were another lengthy activity which took up an afternoon a week. One of the major topics that he was discussing was how to pilot a new manufacture. Most of his time alone was spent working out a big capital proposal for erecting a new plant.

He was out of his office nearly 50 per cent of the time and spent 20 per cent of his time outside the company. He had a variety of contacts outside as he sat on three external committees. One of these was the local productivity committee for his industry. He paid several visits to the parent company.

Mr Salter's job was a much more varied one than Mr Turner's. One reason was that he was managing two different kinds of works producing different products, by different methods of production. Another reason was that he was much more involved in the general management of his company. Much of his time was taken up in acting as a contact point between sales, research and development and purchasing. He may have chosen to emphasise this aspect of the job. Mr Salter's job had become more varied after his company had been taken over by a larger and wealthier organisation, which opened up wider possiblities for expansion.

CYCLICAL WORK PATTERNS

Most jobs involve some element of repetition. This is often associated with a time cycle. The unskilled manual worker may do the same thing every few seconds or every few minutes. The time cycle of a manager's job, where there is one, is likely to be a much longer one. Some managers' jobs may have a daily cycle for some activities, and a weekly or monthly cycle for others. In some jobs the seasonal cycle may have the most effect on the manager's work. In all managers' jobs, particularly middle and senior management, there may be elements that are not repeated.

Few management jobs have a daily cycle, with regular activities taking place each day at the same time. One of the most marked examples of such a job is that of the senior nurse, but then a hospital follows a more rigid timetable than a factory, and nurses are taught to do things at specific times. An observation study of two senior nurse managers showed that both followed a very precise routine, much of it repeated each day.[1] Both had a remarkably similar pattern; for instance, from about 8.30 to 9 a.m. both read the post and discussed it with the nursing administrative staff on duty, together with the arrangements for the day. The day's post always included enquiries about the nurses' training school, applications for posts advertised and requests for references. From about 10.15 to 12.30 both of them interviewed applicants and personally showed them round the hospital. They also normally did ward rounds then. Few managers in industry have such a pronounced daily cycle, though no doubt there are also variations between senior nurses. Amongst the managers who kept the diary, it was the production managers who most often had recurrent daily activities such as a morning production meeting and tours of inspection.

Part of the time cycle of a manager's work may be determined by the job, such as attending a weekly committee meeting or preparing the monthly trading figures; and part may be at his or her discretion.

The existence of regular deadlines is likely to impose a cyclical pattern on work activities. This is most pronounced in journalism, but it is also true to a lesser extent of jobs such as accounting, which entail responsibility for the regular provision of information. Some engineering jobs will also have a cyclical pattern, especially if there are periodic overhauls of major plant. Administrative jobs that involve secretarial duties for committees will have a cycle that is geared to the committee timetable.

In jobs that have a definite cycle of activities there will be considerable differences in how managers will spend their time at different stages of the cycle. This can be illustrated by the variations in weekly figures of an accountant who was in charge of the budgetary control and cost systems departments in a large company. The figures given will be the proportion of time spent in individual weeks, not the proportion for the whole four weeks, as in most of the previous illustrations. The accountant's main work cycle was a monthly one. He started keeping the diary in the first week of the cycle. His diary figures for the first week differed markedly from those for the fourth week.

In the first week he had time to devote to longer-term projects, such as the budget for the next year and a revision of the costing system. Much of this work he did on his own, so in this first week he spent only 42 per cent of his time with other people. His discussions on these projects were with his fellow specialists, with whom he spent 31 per cent of his time in that first week. Many of these discussions were with only one other person at a time. He hardly saw his subordinates that week, spending only 7 per cent of his time with them. In the second week he was extremely busy, especially towards the end of the week, when he was preparing the quarterly figures. He had many more fleeting contacts than in the other three weeks. The third week had no outstanding characteristics. In the fourth week he prepared the monthly report. This was a team effort involving both his subordinates and, to a lesser extent, his colleagues. During that week he spent 82 per cent of his time with other people, nearly all of it in group discussions with his subordinates. All these discussions took place in his own office, so that during that week he worked there almost exclusively.

This accountant is an extreme example of how unreliable figures for one, or even two weeks, can be. The maximum and minimum weekly figures for the time spent alone differed by 47 per cent, and the time spent with subordinates by even more, 75 per cent. The difference is less pronounced if the first two weeks are compared with the last two, but there is still a difference of 30 per cent in time spent alone and of 35 per cent in the time spent with subordinates. There were also big variations in the amount of time spent in his own office and in the proportion of his time with other people that consisted of single discussions as compared with group discussions.

VARIATIONS FROM WEEK TO WEEK

The accountant's pronounced monthly work cycle may have given him unusually large variations from week to week. In the hospital study quoted earlier, the observers felt that one could get a good picture of the senior nurse's job in a week, but that even two weeks – the time they spent observing – was too short a time to understand the job of a hospital secretary. In the sample of 160 managers, how reliable a picture did one week's diary give of how each manager spent his time? We can try to answer this question by comparing the differences in the proportion of time recorded each week for particular headings in the diary.

Figures 5.1 to 5.6 show the difference between the maximum and minimum percentage of total working time spent on a selected number of diary headings. The range and extent of the variations in time spent alone is surprisingly high, as is shown in Figure 5.1, especially when compared with the average time that the 160 managers spent alone, which was 34 per cent. The amount and range of variation in Figure 5.2 is very similar to that in Figure 5.1 which suggests that an increase in the proportion of time that is spent with other people is most likely to be taken up by informal discussion.

One explanation for a very big difference in either the time spent alone or in informal discussions is a cyclical work pattern. Another is some special project or emergency which meant that the manager spent much longer than usual with his subordinates or colleagues. The accountant, described earlier, was one example of a manager

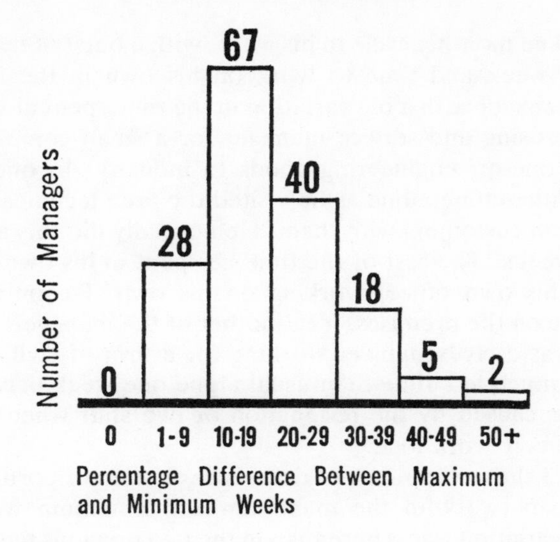

Figure 5.1 Range of differences between the percentage of total working time spent alone in the maximum and minimum weeks

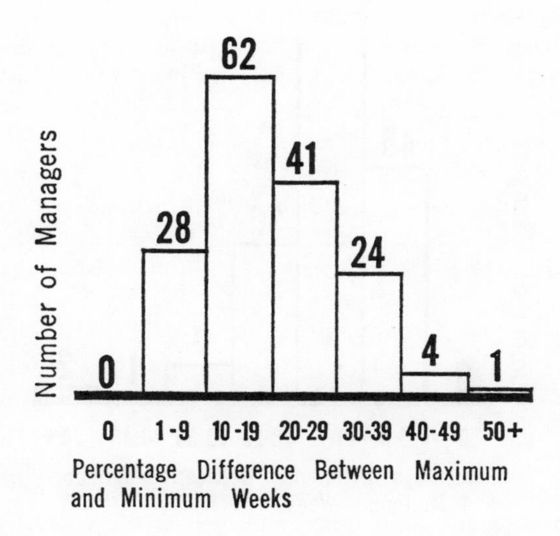

Figure 5.2 Range of differences between the percentage of total working time spent in informal discussion in the maximum and minimum weeks

with a marked monthly cycle to his work, with a burst of team activity in the last week and time to work on his own in the first week. Another manager with a big variation in the time spent alone was the sales, advertising and service manager for a small company selling batch and one-off engineering goods to industry. In one week he spent much less time alone as he visited the area technical salesmen and called on customers with them. He normally did this about once every six weeks. The rest of the time he spent in his own company, mainly in his own office, working on his own. He only had one subordinate on the premises. Yet another of the managers with a big variation was a civil engineer working for a firm of civil engineers, who spent much less time than usual alone one week because there was a panic caused by the resignation of two staff when there was already a heavy work load.

Figure 5.3 shows the range of differences in the proportion of time spent on paperwork in the maximum and minimum weeks. The amount of variation is less here than in the two previous figures, but it is still quite considerable when compared with the average time spent, which was 36 per cent. An unusual increase in writing and

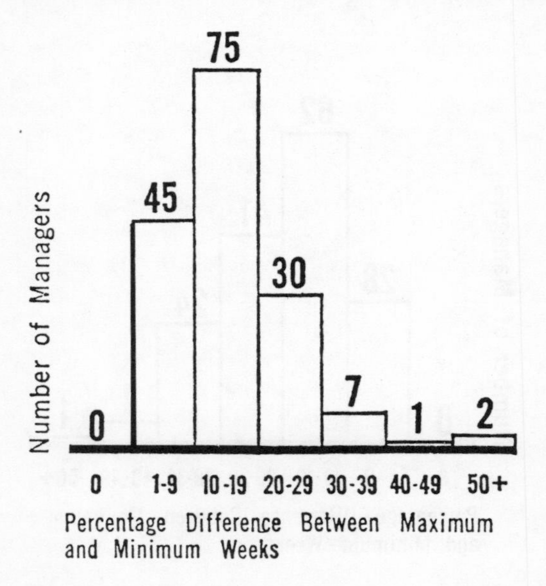

Figure 5.3 Range of differences between the percentage of total working time spent in writing and in reading company material in the maximum and minimum weeks

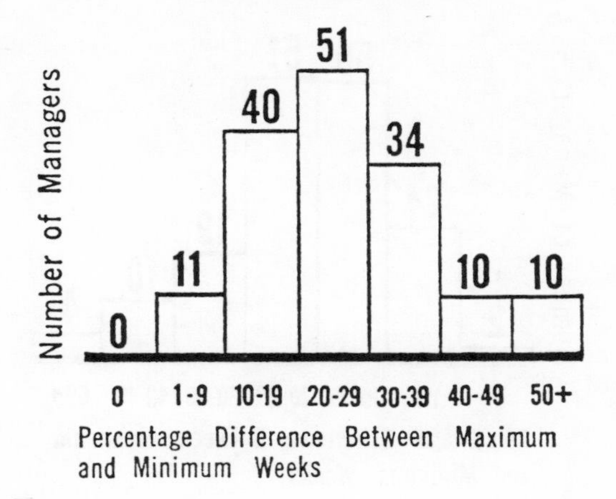

Figure 5.4 Range of differences between the percentage of total working time spent in own office in the maximum and minimum weeks

reading of company material was generally due to writing up some special project, such as the company's annual report. A marked decrease could usually be explained by one of the reasons given above for spending much more time in informal discussions. The amount of time spent on paperwork may also be affected by travelling. One senior design engineer, for example, spent only 19 per cent of his time on paperwork in one week when he was away on a trip for two days. The following week he spent 50 per cent of his time, more than usual, to make up for the previous week. The average of these two weeks would have given a reasonable picture of the amount of time that he normally spent on paperwork, but the average of the first week with the preceding one, or the second with the one that followed it, would have been distorted by the unusually high or low figures.

Figures 5.4 and 5.5 follow each other because they are likely to be connected. Managers spending more time with their subordinates will probably be spending more time in their own office. Managers spending less time are quite likely to be out of the company, or out of the office at a senior meeting.

The average variation is higher in these two figures than in Figures 5.1 to 5.3. This is not surprising as there are many reasons why some managers may have to be away from their company. Managers, such as works managers, who normally spend a lot of time with their

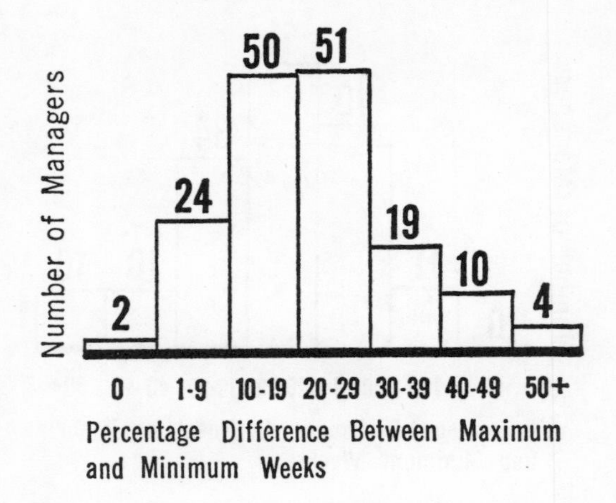

Figure 5.5 Range of differences between the percentage of total working time spent with subordinates in the maximum and minimum weeks

subordinates and have to go away from their company on a special trip will probably, as the diaries showed, spend more time than usual with their subordinates in the first week after their return.

Figure 5.6 gives the variations in the amount of time spent in inspection. It shows a smaller variation than the other figures, but allowance should be made for the fact that managers spent less time in inspection than on the other headings. The large group of managers in the zero column are those who did no inspection. The most common explanation for the few large variations was that a subordinate who usually did much of the inspection was away on holiday or sick, and the boss was doing it instead. Another reason was unusual production problems, which meant that the works manager had to spend more time on the plant.

Jobs that involve travelling will usually have considerable variations in their work activities. Managers may be in their own office for several weeks and then be away for some days at a time. It would be incorrect to base the picture of their work activities on what they were doing while out of the office. It would also be misleading to give a picture merely of what they do when in the office, as this would, for instance, probably show them spending more time with subordinates than if their absences were taken into account. It might also show them spending more time on reading and writing.

Figures 5.1 and 5.6 show that a sample of one week could give a

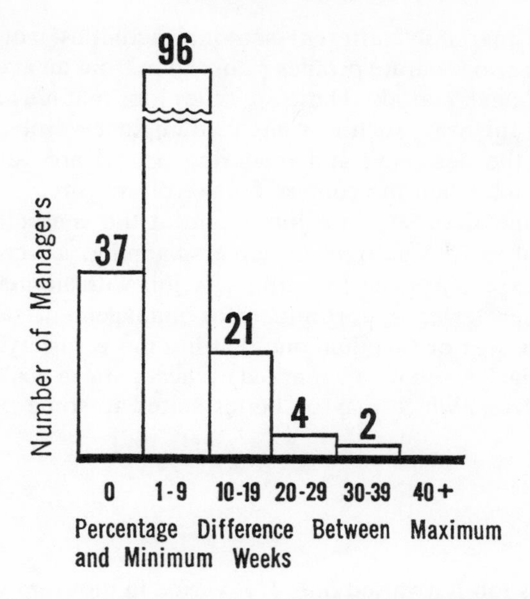

Figure 5.6 Range of differences between the percentage of total working time spent in inspection in the maximum and minimum weeks

very misleading picture of how a manager spends his or her time. Even four weeks may not be an adequate sample for some jobs. This is most likely to be true of jobs that have a cycle longer than four weeks. Production management in a highly seasonal industry, for instance, is likely to have a markedly different pattern at the time of seasonal peak production than at the slack periods. The effects of the seasonal peak will vary from one job to another. We saw in the previous chapter that a brewer's job tends to be much more fragmented in the peak production period than at other times. It is a period of intense activity. By contrast the production manager in an ice-cream factory commented:

> The whole period during which the diary has been kept is the peak production period. This is also the time when Management is under least pressure as budgeting, planning of year's work, maintenance of machines, training of supervisors etc. is completed by March 31st. The summer six months should be a quiet period for Management if planning has been carried out properly.

Jobs with markedly different seasonal activities would be best portrayed by two separate profiles rather than from an average of the peak and off-peak periods. There are other jobs that may also be best portrayed in this way, such as some civil engineers' jobs, where the activities in the designing and tendering period are very different from the period when the contractors are on the site.

The amount of variety in a job is one of the characteristics that should be taken into account in career planning, as it will help to show what experience the job offers. A job with limited variety is likely to offer fewer opportunities for management development after the first year or two than one that has more variety, and hence more challenge. A job with a marked cyclical pattern is likely to have periods of stress, which may be better suited to some personalities than others.

SUMMARY

A manager's job is a varied one. It is varied in different ways: in the place of work, in the contacts, in its activities and in its content. Profiles of two works managers illustrated some of the factors that influence the amount of variety in a job. the main difference between them was that one was in close contact with his colleagues in other departments. He acted as a communication centre for sales, research and development, production and purchasing. The other manager was only concerned with production problems and rarely talked with his colleagues.

Most jobs have some element of repetition. Some, such as journalism, have a definite time cycle. Few management jobs have a daily cycle, although there may be recurrent daily activities such as inspection. More have a monthly or seasonal cycle. Managers in such jobs will spend their time in different ways at different periods of the cycle.

Five figures illustrated the amount of variation in the managers' activities and contacts from one week to another. The extent of these variations in most of the jobs showed that one or two weeks is too short a period to get an adequate record of how the manager spent his time. In some jobs, especially those with a cyclical pattern that is longer than a month, even four weeks is not long enough.

6 Job Profiles

The previous chapters have shown that there were considerable differences in the ways in which the 160 managers spent their time. These variations were so great that it is misleading to talk, as much of the management literature does, about *the* managerial job, or about how the *average* manager spends his or her time. Yet some differences between managers' jobs *are* recognised. Thus we talk of junior, middle or senior managers. We distinguish between works or sales managers, or between staff and line managers. We refer to managers in small, medium or large companies. Sometimes we talk about managers in a particular industry. Although we refer to these different kinds of managers, we are vague about the ways in which they may differ. We know little about differences in the content of their jobs or in the ways in which they spend their time. Hence we fall back upon a very general description of what all managers do.

This chapter suggests a new way of classifying managers' jobs. Unlike the distinctions usually made, it is based on an analysis of how managers spend their time. It is only one of the possible kinds of classification since it is limited to the material contained in the diary. Managers' jobs are so varied and complex that progress towards understanding them requires the gradual building up of a system of classification of the different characteristics of managers' jobs, and of the extent to which jobs vary in their possession of these characteristics.[1]

The data collected in the research were classified by using a special computer program designed by Nigel Howard. This program classifies members of a population, or sample, into groups with common characteristics according to their scores on certain variables. The members of our sample are the 160 managers who kept the diary for four weeks. The twenty-five variables used were derived from the diary entries. The computer began by dividing the managers into two groups, and then into three, and so on up to ten groups. Each grouping was scrutinised to see if it gave a meaningful and distinctive description of different kinds of managers' jobs. The best one was the division into five groups, but it is worth describing the division into three groups as the division into five is a refinement of it. The classification of individual managers into particular groups was compared with the more detailed information available for each manager to see if the grouping of managers appeared to be a reasonable one. In all cases individuals whose inclusion in a particular group at first seemed odd were found to have special features in their job which explained why they were classified in that way. The basis for choosing a particular number of groups and the method of classification used by the computer program are described in Appendix IV.

In the classification into three groups, Group 1 consists of the managers who spent much of their time outside the company, travelling, visiting other companies, attending external committees and receiving visitors from outside the company. They worked the longest hours. Group 2 consists of specialist managers who spent much of their time working by themselves: reading, writing, dictating and calculating. They worked short hours. Group 3 are the average ones in the sample, who spent much of their time talking and listening. Their job was to get other people within their own company to do things. This third group is too large, and contains too many different types of managers, for a three-group classification to be adequate. For this reason Group 3 was subdivided to form two extra groups, making five groups in all.

Now let us look at the characteristics of the five groups of managers. The differences between the groups are shown in a series of diagrams at the end of this chapter. Each group is illustrated by a profile of the way in which the average manager in that group spent his time, which includes all the information discussed in the previous chapters. These profiles are based on individual managers who took part in the research, and whose diary figures were close to the group average. All the details refer to these individuals, but the figures quoted are, unless otherwise stated, the average figures for the group. Usually the figures for the individual portrayed are very similar to that for the group; where this is not true the manager's own figures, together with the figures for the group average, are given, with an explanation of the difference.

Each group has been given a name, which indicates very broadly one of its main characteristics. The managers' names are fictitious, and the descriptions of the companies are general, to ensure anonymity.

PROFILES OF EACH GROUP

Group 1 The Emissaries

The Emissary's work brought him in close touch with the world outside. He spent much of his time away from his company and in talking to people who were not its employees. He often spent several days away, visiting other companies, attending conferences or exhibitions. He worked longer hours than managers in any of the other groups, but this was mainly due to the time spent in travelling and in entertaining. One advantage of his job was that his working day was less fragmented than that of the managers in Groups 3, 4 and 5. Since his work was primarily concerned with people outside the company, he was usually less besieged by subordinates and colleagues when he was in his office. He also had more time to himself than members of any other group, except Group 2, though much of this time was unprofitably spent in car, train or plane.

There are different kinds of Emissaries. The most numerous are those sales managers who had personal contact with customers. Then there are those general managers whose work often took them away from their company, visiting important customers or taking part in professional or trade association activities. Even when they were in their own company, much of their time was spent in contacts with outside people. Group 1 also includes other managers whose work required frequent external contacts, often away from their own company, such as the civil engineers who had to oversee contractors and deal with suppliers. In a larger sample of managers it might, for some purposes, be desirable to subdivide Group 1.

Forty-five of the 160 managers fell into Group 1.[2] These included middle and top managers, in small, medium and large companies, in a wide variety of industries. This group will be illustrated by two examples: the first, a representative portrait of a field sales manager, the second, an individual portrait of a general manager.

(i) *Field sales manager*

Mr Sellars is the general sales manager of a large company making equipment used in offices. He has had his job for three years. Mr Sellars has over twenty managers reporting directly to him, including branch and specialist managers, and a total staff of about 500. He reports to the managing director. He is in his mid-thirties and has been on two specialised management training courses. Mr Sellars is responsible for all aspects of sales and marketing, including initiating the development of new products. He is actively involved in discussions on the technical problems of new equipment. He negotiates personally with large customers. He has complete authority to recruit, promote and dismiss staff as well as to fix their salaries.

The four weeks that he kept the diary was, he said, a typical period, except that during that time he attended a national exhibition that takes place three times a year. He worked 186 hours, an average of 46½ hours a week, of which 8 to 9 hours a week was spent in travelling. These hours, like those of all the managers studied, did not include lunches, except business lunches, nor any other breaks. The length of his working week varied according to the amount of travelling or entertaining that he had to do.

He spent about half his time in his own establishment, mainly in his own office. The rest of his time was divided between calling on important customers, visiting the sales branches, going to the national exhibition for his industry and in travelling. He also took some work home, usually on his return from a trip.

Mr Sellars was alone for just under a third of his working hours, though much of this time was spent travelling. His working day was unfragmented by comparison with managers in Groups 3, 4 and 5. Much of his time was taken up with discussions lasting at least an hour. He had relatively few fleeting contacts, only eight or nine a day, so that he could often work undisturbed when he was in his office. Most of his fleeting contacts were telephone calls with branch managers or customers.

Mr Sellars spent a little more time in group discussions than in conversations with one other person. During the four weeks he had a total of seven hours alone with his boss, the managing director, and another two hours with him and the managing director of a potential customer. He also had one lengthy conversation with his company chairman. He spent about two to three hours a week with his secretary, usually in periods of an hour or more when he returned to his office and cleared his in-tray. His immediate subordinates took about a third of his time. This was longer than the average of 24 per cent for Group 1, but then there were more than twenty people reporting to him. Each one had about an hour and a half alone with him during the four weeks for a general review of the work of their section. He saw some of his salesmen for about two hours a week, usually accompanied by the area sales manager. He spent five hours a week with his colleagues, the other heads of departments, discussing problems of common interest such as the costing of a new product.

Mr Sellars spent eight hours a week with customers, who were his main external contacts. Normally he had one business lunch a week and, during the month that he kept the diary, he spent an evening entertaining an important customer, He also saw one of the component suppliers in order to discuss a new product development that his company was planning. His only other external contacts were competitors whom he met at a trade exhibition. Just over a quarter of Mr Sellars's time was spent on paperwork, including reading, writing, dictating and figure work; correspondence took only an hour a week. He managed to fit in an hour a week for reading trade and professional magazines.

Informal discussions took nearly half of his time. Telephoning averaged only half an hour a day, as most of his calls were fairly short, but naturally he spent longer on the phone on the days he was in the office. Committee meetings were infrequent in his company. In the whole four weeks he spent only three hours in one committee, the monthly management meeting of departmental heads. The average member of Group 1 spent as much time in a week attending committees as Mr Sellars did in the month. Yet it is misleading to talk about the average time that managers in Group 1 spent attending committees, since there were great individual variations. A few attended none, and a few, the general managers, spent more than ten hours a week in committee.

Most of Mr Sellars's time was naturally spent on marketing and sales. His concern with the development of new products brought him in contact with other aspects of the business, particularly production and finance. Personnel activities took up four hours a week; during the time that he kept the diary these included lecturing to sales courses, interviewing prospective salesmen, discussing a new pension scheme and reviewing salaries.

The staple part of Mr Sellars's job consisted of correspondence, the review of recent sales figures, progress meetings with members of his large staff, the selection and training of his staff and discussions with important customers. The two latter usually took him away from his own office. Both his place of work and his contacts were varied. The launching of new products, and the planning of the future advertising programmes, provided the most variety in the content of his work.

(ii) *The public figure*

Group 1 also contains those general managers who spent much of their time with people outside the company who were neither customers nor suppliers. In a sample of 160 middle and top managers one would expect to find, at most, a few general managers who were actively involved in activities outside their company; hence in the profile that follows we shall give the individual's own figures throughout and not attempt a composite portrait.

Mr Outward is managing director of one division of a medium-sized company making batch and one-off goods in the metal industry. It is located in a large town more than 100 miles from London. Mr Outward is in his early sixties. He attended a management course shortly after the war. He has eight immediate subordinates and there are over 300 people in his division. Control over his division is exercised by a divisional board, of which he is chairman.

Mr Outward described the four weeks during which he kept the diary as even busier than usual, but he enjoys it that way. He worked 192 hours, 48 hours a week, a little longer than Mr Sellars. The length of his working week varied from 45 to 54 hours. He travelled by train, and was able to work, so that his working hours included little waste time. He spent about half his time in his own establishment, about a third away from his company and the remainder at the company's head office, which is near by. He worked at home occasionally.

Mr Outward spent 42 per cent of his time alone, more than most members of his group. He spent only 16 per cent of his working day in conversations with one other person at a time. This was because committees took up more than a third of his total working time. There were lengthy monthly meetings of the divisional board and of the main board. He also attended a lot of external committees. He is chairman of the local branch of his professional association and active in the British Institute of Management. He is also chairman of several committees of the trade association to which his company belongs, which meant that he had to travel to London. He is on several advisory committees for the local College of Advanced Technology. He spent just over a quarter of his total working time with people not connected with the company, mainly at his external committees. Most of Mr Outward's contacts were outside the company. He has no boss, and so recorded no time under that heading. Discussions with his immediate subordinates took only 14 per cent of his time, plus a few brief contacts with the more junior members of his division when visiting the office and the factory. During the month he saw no customers and only one supplier.

Writing, dictating and reading took just over a third of his time, longer than most members of Group 1. His mail took much longer than Mr Sellars's, an hour or two a day. He spent only six hours a week in informal discussions. He dislikes social activities, so he left customer entertainment to his sales manager and works functions to his works manager. Inspection took two hours a week, about the average for Group 1.

His work pattern was comparatively unfragmented: one activity often lasted two hours or more. He spent little time on the telephone and had relatively few fleeting contacts, only about three a day. He averaged at least half an hour a day alone without interruptions. Often he had considerably longer.

Mr Outward's job is a very non-specialised one. His work brings him in touch with all aspects of the business, though his main interests are technical. He spent little time on personnel questions – only about two hours a week – and least of all on sales problems. His regular activities were divided between meetings, committees, correspondence and inspection. He had a weekly production conference on work in hand to decide on priorities. He also met the works manager and the cost accountant every week to review performance. Much of his work concerns the industry as a whole. During the month that he kept the diary he wrote a technical report for an international conference of members of his industry. He visited London to discuss a code of practice for the industry and also union demarcation plans.

Group 2 The Writers

This group is markedly different from the others because its members spent more time by themselves in reading, writing, dictating and figurework. Even so, the Writers were only solitary by comparison with other managers. They spent half their time with other people compared with two-thirds to three-quarters for the average member of the other groups. When they were not working alone they were usually talking with one other person. They spent the least time in group contacts. Group 2 spent less than the average time with every type of contact and less than any of the other groups with colleagues, customers and other people outside the company.

Members of Group 2 worked shorter hours than the other groups –

an average of 39 hours a week. These short hours could not be attributed to less travelling, since they spent slightly more time travelling than members of Groups 3, 4 and 5. One reason for the Writers' shorter hours may be that they were more able to control their working day, as they had fewer personal contacts. They were not so much subject to the pressure of day-to-day problems and crises as many of the managers in the other groups.

Group 2 spent about the same amount of time as Groups 3, 4 and 5 within their own establishment, but considerably more in their own office. They rarely had to attend committees, which was one of the reasons why they spent so little time in group contacts. They were more specalised than any of the other groups, though not outstandingly so. Most of their time was spent in their own function.

What kind of managers belonged to this group? It included head office specialists; one would expect to find them spending more time than other managers working on their own. In our sample these were mainly specialist engineering advisers, but some other types of specialist advisers would belong to this group. It also included managers who, although they headed a fair-sized department, were primarily concerned with paperwork, much of which they did on their own. In this category were some of the sales managers who spent their time on the office administration of selling, one payroll manager and a few accountants and company secretaries. What is surprising – and a salutary reminder of the confusion that can be caused by job titles – is the fact that this group contains several production and works managers whose distribution of time between different activities distinguished them from those of their fellow members of the Institution of Works Managers who are found in Groups 4 and 5.

The line managers who belong to Group 2 differed from its other members in two main ways: they spent more of their time with subordinates and they spent more time on personnel. Both may be explained by the fact that they had more staff than the specialist managers in the group. The line managers in Group 2, including the works and production managers, are distinguished from their colleagues in other groups by the much greater amount of time spent in solitary paperwork. Subordinates did not take much less of their time, but they had less contact with people in other departments. The possible reasons for this will be explored in the next chapter.

Group 2 includes thirty-three managers in small, medium and large companies, but the head office specialists are, as one would expect, all in large companies. The other managers come from companies which vary widely both in size and in type of industry. Most of the group are middle managers, but there are a few top managers and some fairly junior technical specialists. This group will be illustrated by two profiles, one of a backroom specialist, the other of a head office specialist adviser. We choose two examples because their jobs are rather different, and in a larger sample of managers Group 2 might be divided into two separate groups. Members of Group 2 differed from each other in the number of their fleeting contacts. The back-room people had very few, whereas some of the head office advisers and some of the line managers had a large number. We shall give the individual's own figures throughout and explain where these differ from the group's average by more than a few per cent.

(i) *The back-room specialist*

Mr Back is an assistant manager in one division of the London-based computing branch of a very large company. He is in his late thirties, a graduate mathematician, and an Associate Member of the Institution of Electrical Engineers. He has been on one company management course for middle managers. He has had his present job for a year, during which time there have been no major changes. Mr Back has six people reporting to him, four of them also graduate mathematicians. These six have no staff of their own, so Mr Back has no other people under his command. He reports to the head of his division in the large computing department. His job is the formulation and specification of the engineering and mathematical requirements of the computer programmes used in planning the most economical development of the company's production. He is responsible for the supervision and technical guidance of his graduate staff who are engaged on programme logical development. He has to coordinate with outside departments on the application of programmes. The four weeks during which he kept the diary were normal.

He worked 153 hours, that is, 38 hours a week, none of it at home. Most weeks he does no travelling and spends no time in social activities at work. As one would expect, Mr Back spent more time in his own office than most managers: he was there for 75 per cent of his working time, and in his own establishment for a further 15 per cent. The remaining 10 per cent he spent either in other parts of the company or outside the company at professional meetings.

He worked alone for 66 per cent of his time, often for an hour or more. He had few fleeting contacts, about four a day. His subordinates were working on long-term tasks and rarely needed to interrupt him with a query. His small amount of contact time was equally divided between single and group discussions.

Mr Back spent four to five hours a week with his boss. This included one long discussion of future plans that also brought him into contact with his boss's boss. Sometimes he joined his colleagues and fellow-specialists from other divisions of the computer department for discussions with his boss. He never talked to them alone. A quarter of his time was spent with his subordinates, often in lengthy discussions with individuals. He had some contact with people in other parts of the company and, at a conference, with computing specialists in other companies. Most of his time with other people was spent in informal discussions. He attended no regular committees, but during the month he went to two special committees, one of them in the computing department and the other involving other departments as well.

When he was alone his time was about equally divided between figure work and writing and reading. Correspondence took a negligible amount of time. Every week he managed to do some professional reading, though this varied from half an hour one week to five hours another.

Mr Back's job was a highly specialised one, more specialised than that of many of the managers in Group 2 and much more specialised than managers in the other groups. He diverged most from the average for Group 2 in the greater amount of time he spent by himself in his own office, in his very unfragmented work pattern and in his small number of fleeting contacts. He spent a little more time with his boss and his subordinates but less with other people. He also spent unusually little time on personnel matters, less than half an hour a week. This is partly due to the fact that he had no authority for the recruitment, promotion, salary increases or discharge of his staff. His job was primarily a research one; his management activities involved the technical supervision of research and the allocation of work.

(ii) *Head-office specialist adviser*

Mr Senter is the chief electrical engineer of a large company in a process industry. He works at the head office, which is in the Midlands. His boss is the chief engineer. Mr Senter is in his late thirties and has had his job for four years. Like Mr Back, he is an Associate Member of the Institution of Electrical Engineers, and has attended a number of company management training courses. He has ten people reporting to him, nine of whom are engineers and the tenth his secretary. There are a further fifteen people under his command.

Mr Senter described his job as having three main responsibilities: (1) making certain that all electrical plant and equipment that is bought is the best value for money; (2) setting and maintaining standards of electrical engineering; and (3) advising on the employment and training of electrical engineers in the company. There were no major changes in his job in the last year. He has authority to hire, fire, promote or transfer, subject to his boss's approval, and can recommend salary increases. The month during which he kept the diary was a normal one.

Mr Senter worked for 165 hours, that is, 41 hours a week, none of it at home. He averaged two to three hours a week travelling and about the same amount of time on social activities with his subordinates and with suppliers. Both these were more than the average for the group and probably explain why he worked slightly longer hours than most of them. Mr Senter spent 81 per cent of his time in his own establishment and 67 per cent in his own office. The rest of his time was divided between visiting other parts of the company and visits outside the company, mainly to suppliers.

Half of Mr Senter's working day was spent alone, a little more than a quarter with one person and the rest in group discussions or committees. His work pattern was more fragmented than that of Mr Back, but he did have opportunities to get on with his work undisturbed. Each week he had three periods alone of half an hour or more – usually quite a lot more – to work in peace, and a further six such periods a week with some brief interruptions. Many of his discussions with other people lasted several hours. He had many more fleeting contacts than Mr Back, about ten a day. Nearly all these were with people inside the company, his subordinates, the electrical engineers in other parts of the company and his secretary, of whom he made good use.

Mr Senter spent only about an hour a week with his boss, the chief engineer. He said that the reason for this well-below-average time for Group 2 was that he was the most senior electrical engineer in the company so that in a technical sense he had no boss. He spent a third of his working time with his subordinates. This high figure is probably explained by the fact that he had ten people reporting to him. More than half of this time was spent talking with subordinates individually. He saw very little of his more junior staff, and never saw them alone. His work brought him into contact with the electrical engineers working in different parts of the company. It also involved meeting suppliers of electrical equipment; few other members of Group 2 had any dealings with suppliers. Mr Senter had no contact with customers.

He spent nearly a third of his time in informal discussions and under an hour a week in internal committees. He attended one monthly committee on engineering policy. He also served on one external public service committee where his specialist knowledge was of value. This took nearly a day a month. His telephone calls were mainly long ones about machinery breakdowns in distant plants. He did no inspection, in the sense used in the diary of a personal tour of workplace. During the month he attended no lectures or conferences. Paperwork, that is writing, dictating, figure work and reading company material, took over a third of his time. An unusually large amount of time – 15 per cent of his total working time – was taken up by reading external matter, including mail from suppliers and trade magazines. Mr Senter said that he had given a great deal of thought to whether it was necessary for him to spend so much time on reading the mail – the average day's mail had fifteen items, with a large tender or specification of twenty to thirty pages every other day – but he had decided that it was a control of the flow and accuracy of work going through his department that he should retain.

Most of Mr Senter's regular activities involved paperwork, which he did in his own office. Each day he read the mail from suppliers and examined specifications. He read file copies of correspondence sent out by his subordinates. He also had quite a lot of regular work that occurred less frequently; for example, he discussed the progress of site work, he checked cost estimates for a new installation, and prepared a report for his boss to present to the next meeting of the board of directors on special items of interest on projects. Most months he spent some time discussing new projects. During the month he was also engaged in a number of special activities, such as an examination of the use of critical path analysis on projects. He also studied the implications of changes in Electricity Board tariffs.

Mr Senter's job was concerned with research and development for new engineering projects, with the efficient maintenance of existing plant and with the purchasing of new plant. His main responsibility was to ensure that the company got the most efficient plant for its needs, and that the plant ran well. This meant that he was intimately involved in the design and specification for new plant, with modifications to existing plant and with queries about the malfunctioning of plant. This work, though specialised, brought him in touch with three management functions: research and development, production, and purchasing. He had no authority to initiate projects that cost money, and for this reason spent very little time on finance, He had nothing to do with sales. Personnel and training questions took up 10 per cent of his time, a little more than the average manager in his group. This was because he had to deal both with the personnel problems of his own staff and with the staffing and training of electrical engineers in the company as a whole. The company runs courses for its managers and Mr Senter was one of the people who was asked to lecture.

Group 3 The Discussers

Each of the other four groups had one or more characteristics which distinguished them sharply from the others. This was not true of Group 3, as the proportion of time that its members spent in different activities was close to the average for the whole sample of 160 managers.

Group 3 are called the Discussers because they spent the most time with other people and with their colleagues, but they are not markedly different from Groups 4 and 5 in the amount of their contact time. They spent the same amount of time in contacts involving two or more people as the average for the whole sample, but more time than that of members of the other groups in conversations with one other person. They could be called the 'horizontal' group because of the amount of time that they spent with their colleagues, that is people reporting to the same boss, and because they spent less time than the average with their own staff. Yet they saw more of their boss than the managers in other groups.

What kind of managers are to be found in Group 3? The group, which is closest to the average figures for the whole sample, contains, as one might expect, a wider variety of managers than the other groups. It includes all four production engineering managers in the sample, several personnel managers with fair-sized departments, most of the accountants and company secretaries, a number of sales managers who spent most of their time in their own office, one works manager and the only merchandise manager in the sample. Group 3 includes 35 managers from small, medium and large companies in a variety of industries. It includes middle and senior managers, but no general managers. Group 3 is illustrated by one profile.

Mr Fellows is the chief accountant of a medium-sized company in the textile industry, which employs about 2000 people. The company is in the north of England. Mr Fellows is a chartered accountant in his mid-forties. He has been in his present job for five years; the main change has been an increase in his staff. His boss is the managing director. He has four people reporting to him and 100 in his department.

Mr Fellows is responsible for the company's financial accounts, periodic profit statements, operating and material control statements, customer's invoicing, the calculation and payment of wages and mechanised accounting. He has complete authority on personnel matters affecting his staff. He described his major activities as follows: discussing with supervisors and subordinates their day-to-day problems so as to maintain an even and punctual flow of work; the preparation of the annual financial accounts; personnel problems; and projects for assessing the relative profitability of products or proposals. The four weeks that he kept the diary were normal, apart from a move to a different office.

He worked 161 hours, that is, 40 hours a week. His normal working day began at 8.30. He lunched from 12.30 to 1.30 p.m. with his fellow managers, which was not classified as work. He finished between 5.15 and 5.30 p.m. He did about an hour's work a week at home. Mr Fellows's company is all on one site and he spent no time travelling. Group 3 managers who were in companies with a number of establishments in different places spent a couple of hours a week travelling in order to visit them. Mr Fellows's working hours included a business lunch every one or two weeks. The Annual General Meeting took place during this month and his social activities included entertaining the Press.

He spent almost the whole of his working time in his own establishment. He spent an unusually large amount of time, 75 per cent, in his own office, compared with an average for the group of 53 per cent. He explained this by the clear glass partition in his own office, which enabled him to see and to sense what was happening in the general office without leaving his desk. His new office is enclosed in solid walls and he found that he now spent more time away from his desk.

Mr Fellows was alone for only a quarter of his working time, in spite of his glass-partitioned office. When he was alone, he was usually able to get on with his work without any interruptions. Each week he had three or four periods alone of half an hour or longer that were undisturbed, and another two interrupted by telephone calls or brief queries from subordinates. He had ten fleeting contacts a day; most of his time spent with other people involved fairly lengthy conversations, usually with one person.

The average manager in Group 3 spent five hours a week with his boss, more than the managers in any other group. Mr Fellows's boss, the managing director, was on holiday during this period; normally he would have had a regular weekly review with him as well as attending the fortnightly executive meeting. Mr Fellows made good use of his secretary, with whom he spent about 40 minutes a day. He usually started the day by looking at his mail and dictating a few letters. This was followed by discussions with his subordinates, both singly in his office, and with several of them in the general office. Altogether he spent about an hour and a half a day with his immediate subordinates, that is, just over a fifth of his time, sometimes in company with some of the more junior members of his department. He spent only a little less time with his colleagues, with whom he discussed both particular problems in their own departments and problems affecting the company as a whole. During the month he had a number of discussions with the works manager and with the sales manager about a tender for a government contract. His concern with costing the profitability of products involved him in discussions with the technical staff.

Mr Fellows had a number of external contacts with whom he spent about three hours a week. He was on the local committees of the Institution of Works Managers and of the Institute of Cost and Works Accountants. Occasionally, he had other contacts outside the company. During the month that he kept the diary he saw local officers of the Transport and General Workers' Union to discuss payment of their members' wages by cheque. He had no contact with customers and only occasionally saw a supplier of office equipment.

He spent two or three hours a week attending committees. These were mainly his external professional committees, as the only internal one was the fortnightly meeting of senior executives. He also attended an *ad hoc* Board of Trade advisory committee in his industry. He spent a little over half his time in informal discussions and just over a third on paperwork. Figurework took two to three hours a week; he was able to delegate most of it. He found time to spend an hour or two a week on external reading, including professional journals.

Mr Fellows's job, as chief accountant of a medium-sized business, and a member of the senior executive committee, brought him into contact with most aspects of the business. His routine activities mainly involved the day-to-day running of his department. Personnel work took about half a day a week. His recurrent, but less frequent activities often concerned other departments. During the month that he kept the diary he discussed the profitability of a product with the technical staff, and a tender for a government contract with the other senior executives. He also talked to shareholders and the Press at the Annual General Meeting. Some of his activities, as one might expect, were concerned with special problems. Two of these, during the four weeks, were making arrangements for payment of wages by cheque and deciding the recruitment policy for the mechanised accounting section.

Group 4 The Trouble-shooters

Group 4 are the managers with the most fragmented work pattern. This was shown both by the frequency of their diary entries and by their large number of fleeting contacts. This fragmentation arose because they, far more than the managers in the first three groups, had to cope with crises. Even though they may have planned carefully to avoid trouble, much of their time was spent dealing with problems which, when they arose, needed a speedy solution. The repercussions of a failure to solve problems were likely to be more rapid and dramatic than they would be in other departments of the business.

Group 4 could also be called the 'man managers' as they spent longer with their subordinates than any other group and longer than any, except Group 5, with the more junior people under their command. Their internal contacts were mainly within the straight-line hierarchy: they spent less time than the sample average with any of the other people in the company. Their main external contacts were with suppliers, with whom they spent more time than any of the other groups.

There is one further way in which Group 4 managers differed from those in other groups, that is in the relatively large proportion of their time that they spent on inspection. For the other managers this was a small part of their work, but for the Trouble-shooter it occupied more than an hour a day. Most of the members of Group 4 were responsible for a physical area, which they inspected themselves every day.

Most of the works managers come in Group 4. The remainder, with a few exceptions, are in Group 5, along with some production managers. Group 4 contains several factory managers and some who are called works manager, but whose responsibilities are those of a factory manager. There are a few engineering managers who spent a lot of time with their subordinates and on inspection. Group 4 also includes a few general managers of small companies or subsidiaries, who spent nearly all their time in their own company, and who were mainly concerned with works management. The group contains thirty-three managers from small, medium and large companies in a wide variety of industries. It includes works managers in charge of one-off, batch, mass and process production.

Mr Mann is the factory manager of a medium-sized works in London. It is part of one division of a large company. The factory is mainly engaged in mass production, with a small amount of batch production. Mr Mann, who is in his mid-forties, has had his present job for four years. During that time he has been given greater autonomy and responsibility for results. He is a Member of the Institution of Mechanical Engineers. He has eight people reporting to him and a total staff of about 700. His boss is the general manager of the product division, which is composed of a number of factories.

Mr Mann is the general manager of his factory with full local responsibility for results. He has reporting to him the following: works manager, production controller and buyer, the works engineer, commercial manager, accountant, personnel officer and the quality measurement service. He has full authority for all hourly-paid workers and junior staff, but must get the approval of head office for the recruitment, promotion and discharge of other staff. He must also get head office approval for capital expenditure over a modest figure, for price changes on large annual contracts and for product changes. He sets and controls priorities of projects, subject to consultation with head office. The four weeks that he kept the diary were normal except that they included a conference that occurs biannually.

He worked 170 hours, an average of 42½ hours a week, varying from 39 to 45 hours. Only once did he take work home. He spent 84 per cent of his time in his own factory. He left it to visit other factories in the same product division, to pay an occasional visit to head office or to go to a conference or exhibition. All these were also in London, so that he only spent a couple of hours a week in travelling. His social activities took up 12 hours during the month, more than is usual for him, as he went to the company's annual dance for senior executives. He would spend longer on social activities than most members of the group as he is president of the sports and social club in his own factory.

Mr Mann had a very fragmented working day. Although he had slightly more time alone than members of Groups 3 and 5, he had few opportunities to work undisturbed. Twice during the week he had half an hour or more entirely to himself. These were his best opportunities for getting down to difficult jobs on his own. His other periods alone were frequently interrupted by fleeting contacts. He managed to record sixteen of these each day, but said that he may have missed some in the pressure of work. Most of his activities during the day lasted under an hour, with the exception of one or two discussions each day that lasted an hour or more.

Mr Mann spent a little more than a third of his time with his subordinates, which was equally divided between individual and group discussions. He saw his junior staff at works committee meetings, social functions and on tours of inspection. He rarely saw any of them on their own. His boss took up an average of three hours a week, but some weeks they spent considerably longer together and in others they only talked on the telephone. Mr Mann spent more than two days during the month with his fellow factory managers. This was more than twice as long as usual, as it included the biannual two-day conference for factory managers in the company to meet top management. Discussions at this particular conference centred on new machine developments and on personnel problems. He spent half a day to a day a month with visitors from head office and longer talking to them on the telephone.

Unlike the average manager in his group, Mr Mann spent no time with suppliers. He leaves this to his buyers. He believed that he should have regular personal contact with his principal customers and some contact with the smaller ones, so he usually spent half a day to a day a month with important customers, always accompanied by his commercial manager.

Mr Mann spent more than 40 per cent of his time in informal discussions. Committees took up only 7 per cent of his time, less than half a day a week. He held a weekly production committee to coordinate sales, production and labour. He also took the chair at the monthly works committee meeting, and at the quarterly meetings of the organisation and methods committee. Inspection took 16 per cent of his time as he inspected most of the works every day. He spent 20 per cent of his time on paperwork and also managed to do a little external reading. He attended no lectures during the month, though he does occasionally lecture to company trainees.

Part of Mr Mann's time was spent in regular activities such as inspection of the works, discussions with staff on day-to-day problems, and reading copies of all outgoing mail. Then there were regular but less frequent activities, such as preparing the targets for the next year, seeing important customers and chairing the works committee. Part of Mr Mann's time was also spent discussing the special problems that arose. During the month he was concerned with the technical and economic feasibility of a new product design, the cost of a new engineering project, the action that should be taken to combat the introduction of a new product by a competitor, and the preparation for marketing a new product.

Mr Mann had a very clear picture of what his job as a factory manager involved. He said that he should interpret instructions from head office for local implementation and feed back information to head office. He must agree commercial production and cost forecasts and watch daily and monthly performance against the forecasts. He believes in promoting direct personal contact between his staff and himself, but took care not to upset the organisational channels. He spent nearly a quarter of his time on personnel matters, double the average for the group. This reflected his own belief in the importance of paying a great deal of attention to personnel and to the interplay of personalities. He spent more time on production than on any other aspect of the business, but his job as factory manager, in charge of departmental heads for all the main functions, brought him in touch with nearly all aspects of the business.

Group 5 The Committee-men

Group 5 differs markedly from the other groups in two respects: one, its wide range of internal contacts and two, the large amount of time its members spent in group discussions. The committee-men had the widest range of internal contacts because their job, more than that of any of the other groups, involved them in both horizontal and vertical contacts. They had few contacts outside the company. Half their working day was taken up with discussions with more than one person; for most of them this meant that a lot of time was spent in committees. They also differed from other groups in spending more time on personnel work.

Managers in this group worked for large companies. Seven of the fourteen who make up this small group come from the production side of the same company. The seven bridged three levels of production management, from the works manager downwards. Most of the group are production or works managers. They differed from their counterparts in Group 4 in their less fragmented work pattern, their wider range of internal contacts, and in the much larger proportion of their time that was spent in multiple contacts, usually in committees.

There are three production specialists in the group who had few or no subordinates. They belong to this group because of the wide range of their contacts and the amount of time that they spent in multiple discussions, usually in committees.

The group also includes one accountant whose work brought him into contact with a wide variety of people in his company. He was a departmental head in the accounts department of a large food company. He had eight people reporting directly to him and 150 in his department. His job had some resemblance to that of a production manager as he was responsible for the day-to-day administration of the mechanised department that produced all invoices and credit notes and dealt with the related ledger-posting and marketing statistics.

Membership of this group was determined partly by size; only managers who worked for large companies belonged to it. There was some indication that the method of production might also be a factor in determining membership. Nine out of the eleven works and production managers who worked in process industries were in Group 5 and none of the small number who worked in mass production industries. Numbers employed in the works, type of production, and company policies are likely to be three factors that help to determine to which group a works manager will belong.

Mr Meeting is the works manager of one division in the Midlands of a very large company in the heavy engineering industry. (This is not the company that contributed seven members to Group 5.) He is 35, a graduate engineer who has had advanced training in management. He has had his present job just over two years. He has eleven immediate subordinates and over 1000 under his command. He reports to the general works manager of the division. He is responsible for all aspects of works management in his large unit,

with the exception of works services. The major change in his job during the last year has been the evolution of self-contained, accountable product divisions within the company. This has resulted in a greater proportion of his time being spent with colleagues, such as the chief engineer, sales manager and contracts manager, in order to establish common policies for the division.

He worked 166 hours during the four weeks, an average of 41½ hours a week, with little variation from week to week. His normal day started at 8.30, sometimes a little earlier. He worked till 1 p.m. and took an hour and a quarter for lunch. He rarely recorded a working lunch, though when lunching with colleagues the conversation sometimes turned to work. He worked till about 5.30 p.m., but occasionally stayed later for an evening meeting.

Mr Meeting spent 86 per cent of his time in his own works, and nearly half in his own office. The rest of his time was divided between visiting other parts of the company and attending a trade exhibition in London. The latter boosted his travelling time to 12 per cent, more than usual, and greater than the group's average of 5 per cent.

He spent just over a quarter of his working time by himself. His working day was less fragmented than that of Mr Mann. Only once or twice a week was he alone and undisturbed for half an hour or more. On most days he also had one period alone of at least half an hour, but this was interrupted by telephone calls, most of them initiated by himself. His door and telephone were guarded by a secretary to protect him from too-frequent interruptions. He had fewer fleeting contacts per day than Mr Mann, an average of twelve a day, of which nine were telephone calls, compared with sixteen for Mr Mann. During the month he had only eight activities, including committees, that took two hours or longer, and a further nineteen that took between one and two hours. Hence most of his time was spent in activities lasting under an hour.

His major activity was group discussions, which took up half his time. Some of these were informal, but a fifth of his time was spent in committees. He went to six committees, none of them outside the company. The most frequent was an internal progress meeting, held once a week, but which he did not always attend. There was a divisional management committee that met once a month, plus *ad hoc* sessions as required on special topics. A central management committee, composed of head office and divisional management, met every three months. The development committee, consisting of divisional management, senior engineers and product staff, had a series of meetings when necessary. Such a series was held the previous month, when he spent even longer in committees. There was also a two-monthly progress meeting with the representatives of the principal customer. There was a six-weekly meeting on project management techniques, attended by members of his own company and by managers from another company. In addition he chaired the monthly meetings of the accident prevention committee and of the foremen's association.

He spent an unusually large amount of time with his subordinates – half his total working time. This was considerably more than the average of 34 per cent for the group. This is explained partly by the fact that two members of the group had no subordinates and one had only one, and partly by the fact that Mr Meeting had eleven people reporting to him directly. Most of his discussions with subordinates took place at informal meetings and committees, but he spent a fifth of his time in talking with them individually.

He also spent an unusually large amount of time with his junior staff, 25 per cent, compared with the group average of 14 per cent. One reason for this was his practice of contracting the lines of communication to try to offset the problem of communications passing through a number of levels of supervision. When he wished to deal with a question affecting a section which was the responsibility of one of his subordinates, he usually had both him and his section chief in together. He did this most often when dealing with trade-union matters, where first-hand information was especially important.

Mr Meeting spent an average of four hours a week with his boss, but most of this was in company with other people. He spent only an hour or two a week with his secretary, mostly in brief exchanges. He had extensive contacts with other people in the company. There were four functional managers, the sales manager, the contracts manager, the chief engineer and himself, all of whom were responsible for the conduct of the business of the division. He spent nearly a fifth of his time with these colleagues, formulating and coordinating the division's policies. Other people in the company also occupied about a fifth of his time. These were mainly members of functional service departments, such as maintenance, accounts and organisation and methods, that did not come under his control.

External contacts took up little time. He spent a few hours each week with customers and one with suppliers. He had little contact with other people outside the company, apart from trade-union officials.

Paperwork, which included writing, dictating, figurework and reading, took 29 per cent of his time. He usually found time to spend an hour or two a week on technical or professional reading. He spent less time on inspection than Mr Mann, about three hours a week, but he did not try to inspect most of the works each day.

His regular activities consisted of works inspection, progress meetings and discussions with subordinates on short-term problems, many of which were only reported to him for information. All these regular activities involved contact with other people, usually in group discussions. His major preoccupation at the time he kept the diary was with longer-term planning for expansion, coupled with a reorientation of the organisation towards larger-scale production of a smaller variety of equipment. As a member of the management team he often initiated policy-making sessions on sales or development policy, on new projects or on the extension of existing projects. During the four weeks one of his special activities was planning new office accommodation – a surprising number of the managers who kept the diary recorded a similar activity.

Mr Meeting, like Mr Mann, was concerned with the general conduct of the business, and so delegated more production matters than works managers who were concerned only with production. The work of both managers covered many aspects of management. Both Groups 4 and 5 included works or production managers whose jobs were more narrowly restricted to production. Mr Meeting, unlike Mr Mann, was not himself responsible for the success of the division: the sales manager and the chief engineer were his colleagues, not his subordinates. Sales and finance occupied little of his time; the accounting organisation was centralised. Mr Meeting spent 16 per cent of his time on personnel matters. In his company line management was expected to handle union negotiations personally, not to delegate them to industrial relations specialists.

Mr Meeting is typical of members of this group in taking part in a variety of discussions, both formal and *ad hoc*, with managers and employees from a number of different levels. His production progress meetings included people from two or three levels. There were meetings with his immediate colleagues, and with head office to discuss developments and progress. Much of his time alone was spent either preparing for the more technical meetings or writing up reports on some of the union negotiations.

COMPARISONS OF THE FIVE GROUPS

Comparative figures for the average member of each of the different groups are given in the following diagrams. Only the most important differences are illustrated. The first figure shows where the managers in the different groups worked. It may be remembered that Group 1 was called the Emissaries, Group 2 the Writers, Group 3 the Discussers, Group 4 the Trouble-shooters and Group 5 the Committee-men. Figure 6.1 illustrates how different members of Group 1 were from the other groups in their places of work, and shows how much longer those in Group 2 spent in their own office. It shows that managers in Groups 2 to 5 spent a similar amount of time in their own establishment. This was rather less than one might expect, but the figure may be reduced by the large proportion of managers in the sample who worked for companies with a number of different establishments.

The second set of diagrams, Figure 6.2, shows how each group of managers divided their time between solitary work, conversations with one person and discussions with a number of people together. It reveals two main points of difference: one, the large amount of time that the managers in Group 2 spent by themselves, and two, the fact that those in Group 5 spent half their time in group discussions.

Figure 6.3 shows the average time that each group spent with different categories of people. The dotted line is the average time for all the groups, that is the total sample. A comparison of the length of the bar for one of the groups with the dotted line will show how far the groups' average time differed from that of the average for the whole sample.

Each bar is divided into two: the shaded portion is the amount of time spent in discussions with one person at a time in that category, and the unshaded portion is the time spent in discussions with more than one other person present, called group discussions. It will be noted that the unshaded portion is usually longer than the shaded portion. This may seem unexpected, since we know that the whole sample spent, on average, almost exactly the same amount of time in single discussions as in group discussions. The explanation is in the problem of classifying group discussions when people from more than one category of contacts are present. Discussions with one other person created no problems; if a manager was talking with one of his subordinates this was simply regarded as a single contact with a subordinate. A manager who took part in group discussions with

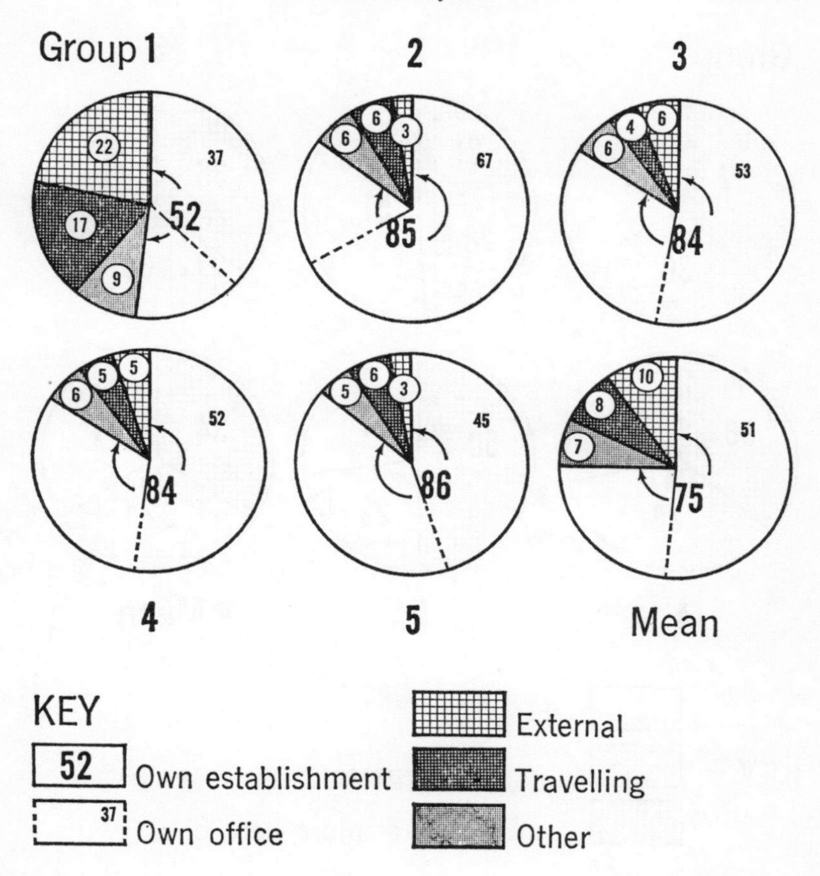

Figure 6.1 Percentage of total working time spent by each group in different places of work

people who were classified in different categories of contacts had his time recorded in two ways. For example, a manager who spent an hour with a subordinate, a colleague and a customer would be recorded as having worked for one hour by attending a group discussion. But he would also be recorded as having spent one hour in a group discussion with a subordinate, one hour in a group discussion with a colleague and one with an external contact. This hour would, therefore, form part of the unshaded portion of the bar for subordinates, for colleagues and for external contacts.

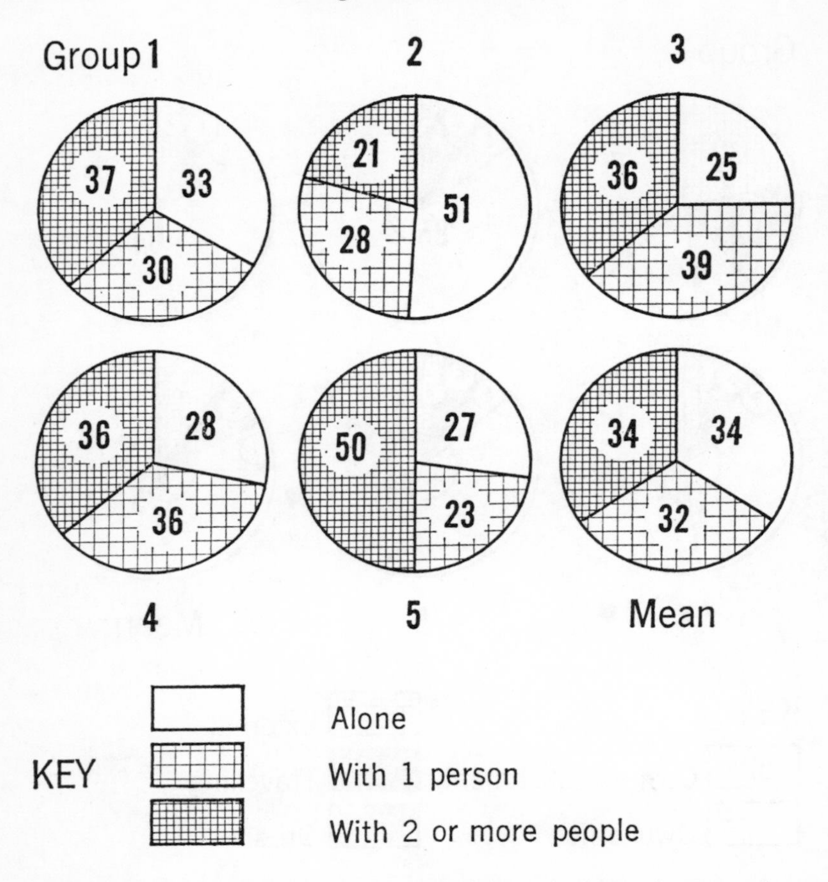

Figure 6.2 Percentage of total working time spent by each group alone, with one person, and with more than one

We can see from Figure 6.3 that members of Groups 4 and 5 spent from 9 to 14 per cent more time with their subordinates than members of the other groups. The average amount of time that members of Group 5 spent with subordinates would have been still higher but for the fact that this small group of fourteen people contains the two managers in the sample who had no subordinates. Figure 6.3 clearly illustrates the range of internal contacts of members of Group 5, the Committee-men, and the larger amount of time that members of Group 3, the Discussers, spent with their

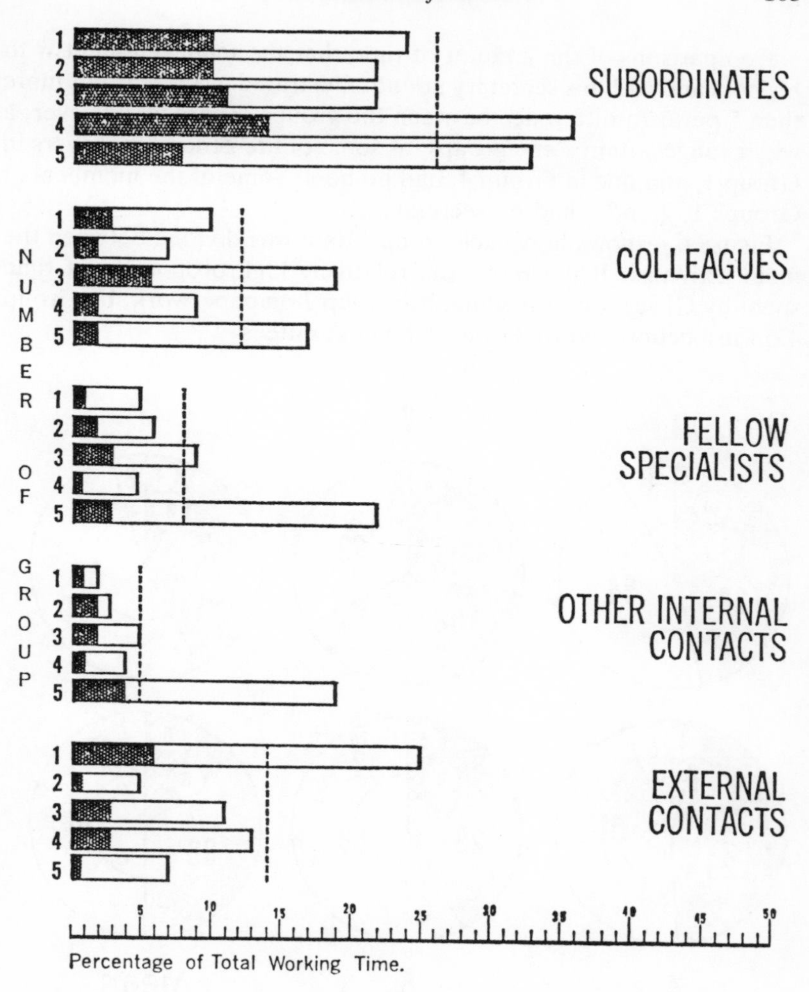

Figure 6.3 Percentage of total working time spent by each group with different categories of people

colleagues. It shows the importance of external contacts for the Emissaries of Group 1. It may be remembered that Group 2, the Writers, spent least time with other people. Figure 6.3 shows that their contact time with their subordinates was not much below the average for the whole sample, but that they spent the least time with colleagues and with external contacts.

Comparisons of the amount of time that the manager spent with his boss and with his secretary are not illustrated as there is not more than 5 per cent difference between the groups. There is, however, a wider range within some groups, as some of the general managers in Group 1, and one in Group 4, had no boss. Some of the members of Groups 1, 2 and 3 had no secretary.

Figure 6.4 shows how each group's time was divided between the main activities. It illustrates the relatively high proportion of time spent by Group 1 in travelling, by Group 2 on paperwork, by Group 4 on inspection and by Group 5 on committees.

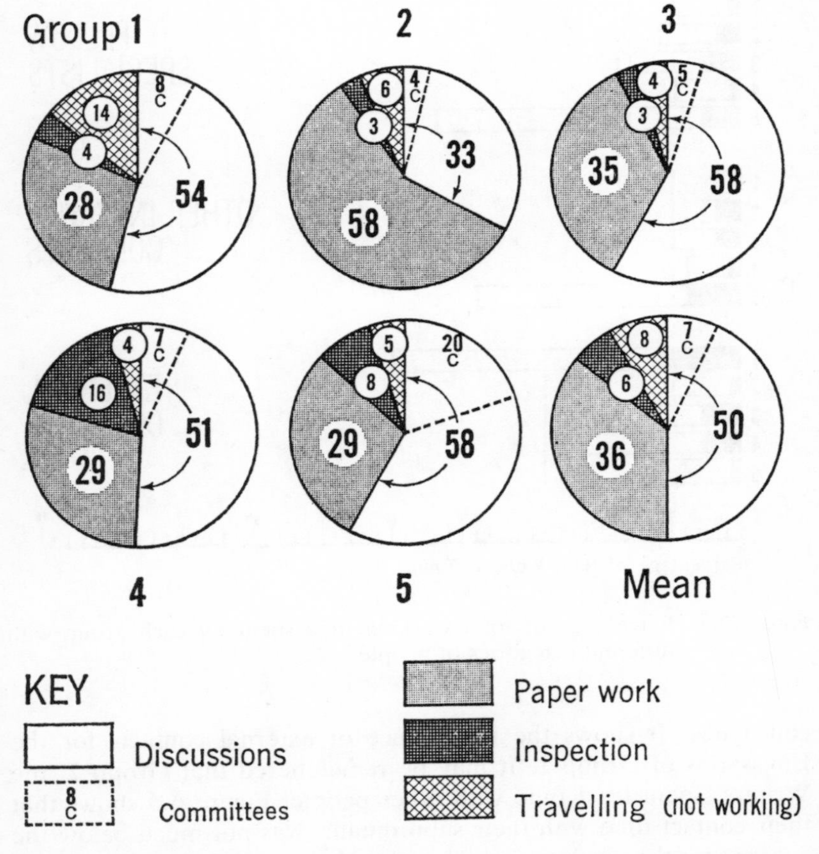

Figure 6.4 Percentage of total working time spent by each group in different activities

The last set of diagrams, Figure 6.5 gives three measures of the amount of fragmentation of the working day, which were discussed in Chapter 4. The first diagram, which gives the average number of diary entries per day, shows that Group 4 was clearly the most fragmented. The second diagram, which gives the average number of

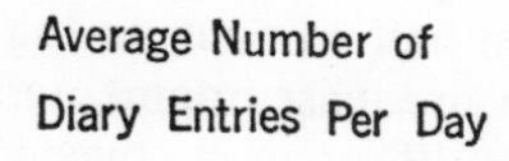

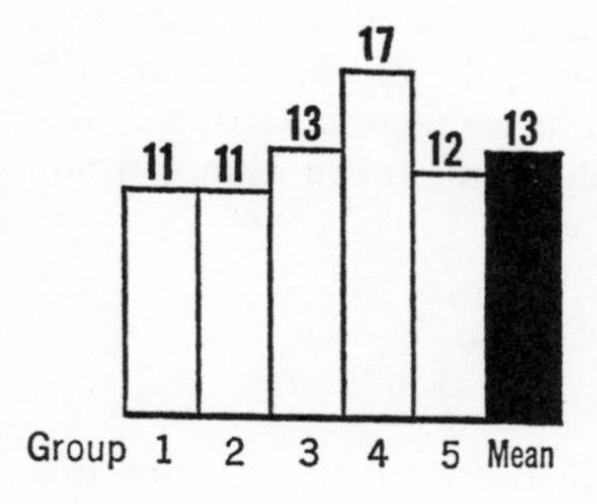

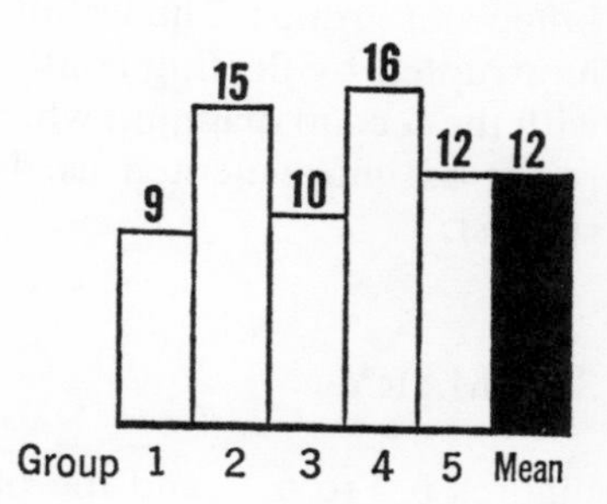

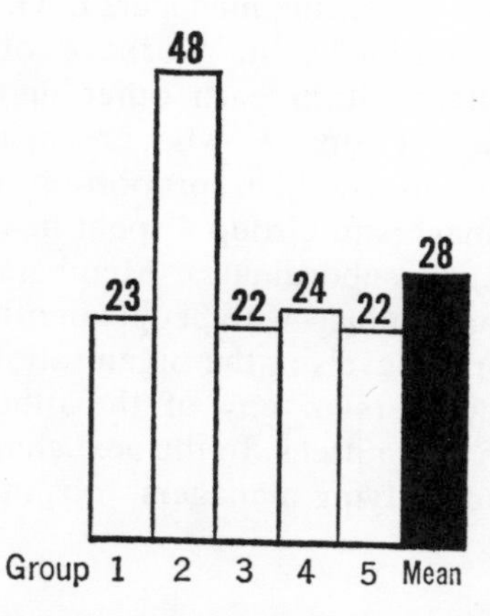

Figure 6.5 Three measures of the fragmentation of each group's working day

fleeting contacts per day, also shows Group 4 as the most fragmented, but only slightly more so than Group 2. It is likely, however, that members of Group 2, who led less hectic lives than those of Group 4, were able to record their fleeting contacts more accurately. It was some of the members of Group 4 who said that they had not been able to record them all. The third diagram, which gives the number of periods alone of at least half an hour during the four weeks, shows that Group 2 was much the least fragmented by this measure, and that there was not much difference between the other four groups. The last diagram includes periods alone that were interrupted by fleeting contacts. It should, therefore, be compared with the second diagram; when this is done we see that Group 2's day is not as unfragmented as the third diagram, taken alone, would suggest.

SUMMARY

Figures 6.2 to 6.4, and the profiles that preceded them, show that one can classify the managers' jobs into different groups according to the relative proportion of time spent on different activities. Groups 1 and 2 are the most distinctive. Groups 3, 4 and 5 were formed by subdividing Group 3. Members of Group 1 are outward-oriented. Their workplace and their contacts were often outside the company. Members of Group 2 spent about half their time in solitary paperwork. The main job of the managers in Groups 3, 4 and 5 was to supervise and coordinate the work of other people in the company. They differed from each other in the nature of their contacts. Members of Group 3, who are nearest to the sample average, spent a relatively high proportion of their time with colleagues. The managers in Group 4 spent nearly all their internal contact time with their subordinates. Members of Group 5 had a wide range of internal contacts with people in other departments and in a variety of different levels in the organisation. They spent much more time than members of any of the other groups in group discussions, often in committees. In the next chapter we shall look at the implications of classifying managers' jobs in this way.

7 Implications of Job Types

Management literature has usually discussed management as if it was a single activity that required uniform abilities and a common body of knowledge. One aim of this book is to argue that we should pay more attention in management development to the differences between managers' jobs. The research that has been described sought to discover some of the similarities in, and some of the differences between, managers' jobs by analysing how 160 managers spent their time for four weeks. Chapters 2 and 4 demonstrated how widely managers may vary in the way they spend their time. The differences are sometimes so great that they show how misleading it can be to talk about the manager's job, or about how the average manager spends his time. Chapter 5 showed that managers' activities may also vary considerably from one week to another, so that managers' jobs should be studied for a minimum of three to four weeks. The variations were most marked in jobs that had a pronounced time-cycle. Jobs with a seasonal pattern would need to be studied over a longer period.

Chapter 6 classified the 160 managers into job types on the basis of the differences in the ways in which they spent their time. The cluster analysis used for the computer programme indicated five job-types. This is not, of course, a definitive classification. Other types of classification can, and should, be made of other aspects of manager's jobs, as the author did in a later study.

What factors determined how these managers spent their time, and hence the group to which each belonged? The composition of the groups should help us to answer this question, though many factors that may be important, such as the type of market or the nature of the production process, could only be studied in a specially selected sample. Broadly, there are three possible explanations: job, organisation and individual. The way in which the managers spent their time may have been determined by the kind of job that they had. It may have been determined by the kind of organisation for which they worked – which may in itself be a reflection of many influences – or it may have been determined by their own individual ways of doing their jobs. One would expect all three factors to have an influence on how a manager's time was distributed. Which was the most important in determining the group to which a manager belonged? When we look at the composition of each group we find that the main difference between them is the type of job, and in particular, the function in which the manager works. If the differences had been primarily due to individual or to organisational variations, the composition of the groups would not have been a predominantly functional one. Most of the sales managers were in Group 1, nearly all the works managers in Groups 4 and 5 and the accountants, with one easily explained exception, in Groups 2 and 3. Group 2 consisted of those specialist staff who spent much of their time on paperwork rather than in personal persuasion and of line managers who worked mainly in their own offices and had little contact with other departments. Group 3 was a more mixed group, which was distinguished most by the types of jobs that it did not contain, that is, general managers, sales managers and works managers. In general, some specialist posts excepted, works managers and sales managers differed most from other management jobs and most from each other.

Managers in the same function were not, however, always classified in the same group. Group 2 contained a few works and sales managers and some senior accountants, though most of their fellows were in other groups. These individual differences show that a purely functional classification would be inadequate. A study of the information about the jobs of the line managers in Group 2 suggested that the differences in the ways in which they spent their time compared with the other line managers was due mainly to the nature of their job, rather than to the way in which they did it. The job of the sales managers in Group 2, unlike that of the sales managers in Group 1, for instance, was primarily an administrative one.

Some of the factors, apart from function, that affected how the managers spent their time, could be discovered by comparing diary figures with the more detailed information about the job. One factor was the extent to which they were involved in the general management of the company, which in itself may have had a number of possible explanations, including how the company was organised and individual choice. Some of the senior line managers were almost exclusively concerned with their own department. Others in the same function and at the same level were involved in the general management of the company. They tended to spend more time with other people, and more time with people outside their own department, than the others. This may have reflected the individual's choice. Some managers take more interest in what is happening in other related functions, while others concentrate more on their own department.

Comparisons were made to see whether there was a relation between the size of the company, or works, as measured by the number of its employees, and the time that the senior line managers spent with other people. This was relevant to understanding the line managers in Group 2 who were distinguished by their low contact time. There seemed to be a tendency for the contact time to increase with the number of employees, but the result was only statistically significant (at 0.01) for senior accountants. (The senior accountants who worked for companies or subsidiaries employing fewer than 1000 people were compared with those in companies with more than 1000 employees.)

It is not possible in this study to make an adequate assessment of the effects of differences of level in the hierarchy in determining job types, because the managers came from many different companies, which made it difficult to match levels, and because almost all were middle or top managers. Differences in level did not seem to be a factor in the composition of the groups, though it might be a factor in a classification based on a different type of information.

What are the implications of job types for management training? There are two main implications that stem from the differences between managers' jobs as shown by this research. The first is the need to re-examine the basis for deciding that a management training course is suitable for one manager and not for another. The present procedure for most management courses is to send to the same course people who are at roughly the same level, such as middle management, but from many different types of job. It is implied that all managers at a particular level, junior, middle or senior, will be suited by the same management course. This may be true for certain types of courses, such as internal company courses where the primary aim is to tell managers about the company and to enable them to meet a variety of their fellow-managers. Such courses, however, often have other aims than the 'meet your company' one; aims that may be far more relevant for some of the managers than for others. The composition of the different job types suggest that, except for certain purposes, level may not be the best criterion for determining which managers should attend which courses.

The second implication of job types for management training is the need to develop some new types of course. There should be more courses that seek to tackle the particular problems of particular types of jobs. To run such courses effectively, training managers will need much more information about the nature and problems of individual jobs in their organisation than they are likely to have at present.

The two most important differences between managers' jobs shown by this study are the contacts that the job involves,[1] and the work pattern, as shown by the amount of fragmentation of the working day. Further research would no doubt indicate other differences that should be taken into account. The first difference, that between the frequency, range and type of managers' contacts, is relevant to the section of many management courses that is devoted to human relations, communications and trade unions. It can be argued that all managers should benefit from such sessions since all have to get things done by other people; all too have to give and receive information. Some of the problems of communication are the same in different types of job but by no means all. The people to whom the managers talk, and the form these contacts take, vary considerably from one job to another. The human relations content of many management courses seems to be designed for those who have many subordinates with whom they have difficulty in communicating and whose attitudes they have difficulty in understanding. Yet many managers' jobs pose different problems in dealing with other people and require different skills. The manager, for example, who heads a small specialist section may work more as a team leader than as a manager. Much of the content of some human relations courses may be of little relevance. One crude, but useful, distinction that shows some of the differences in the human relations problems of different jobs is in the proportion of time that is spent on personnel matters. This is much greater in some jobs and in some organisations than in others. Some of the managers studied spent little or no time on personnel problems, either because they were in charge of a small specialist group or because they had no authority to hire, fire, promote, transfer or reward their staff. For most of them, and for some of the other managers, information about trade unions would have no direct relevance for their work. Managers, like those in Group 5, who spend a lot of time at meetings with people from different levels and departments will require different skills from those whose contacts are mainly with their subordinates or with one person at a time. It seems desirable that human relations courses should take into account the differences in the skills required by managers with different types of contacts.

The second main difference between the managers' jobs studied was in the amount of fragmentation. Some jobs were much more fragmented than others. At one extreme were those that were characterised by a large number of fleeting contacts, by short periods spent in any one activity, by little time alone and that broken up into short periods. At the opposite extreme were jobs that allowed their occupants to plan their day with the likelihood that they would be able to keep to their plan. Such jobs were relatively unfragmented, with long periods of time spent in the same activity. Managers in the first type of job had to face many problems that differed from those in the second type.

One of the most important implications of the research is the possibility that some management jobs have distinctive problems that management trainers need to understand if they are to provide the most useful types of courses. Since one common aim of management training is to try to improve management efficiency, management development should include the efficient use of the manager's own time. The problems of trying to organise one's time efficiently are much greater in some jobs than in others. Jobs that permit their holders to plan their work with a reasonable hope that they will be able to keep to their plan are not difficult to organise efficiently, provided that the manager has learned to delegate. Jobs such as those held by the managers in Group 4, which are highly fragmented, can encourage a grasshopper approach to work. Because their occupants must so often switch their attention from one problem to another, it can become a habit that is difficult to avoid when it is not necessary. As one of the managers taking part in the research said: 'I was appalled at the grasshopper way in which I work.' It is a temptation in highly fragmented jobs to make the current problems a perpetual excuse for postponing consideration of the long-term ones. Management training for the holders of such jobs should try to help them to overcome the particular hazards to efficiency that are characteristic of their jobs by giving them special training in the defining of job objectives, in setting work priorities and in the methods of checking that they are keeping them. Another hazard to efficiency that characterises some jobs is the temptation to become merely a post office. This is a danger in jobs that require liaison between groups. The temptation is greatest where there is an element of conflict between the groups.

The concept of job types, which are not synonymous with functions or levels, indicates the need for a new approach to management development and career planning. There is a need for those concerned with management development to study the job-types in their own organisation, to learn more about the kinds of experience that these can provide and to understand the particular efficiency hazards that may be associated with different job types. When this information is available it will be easier to decide which jobs offer the best preparation for top management; some may even provide experience that is the opposite of what is required at a more senior level. Such information should be taken into account in career planning and in training for promotion. There is a need for special courses that concentrate on the problems met by each job type. There may also be a need for courses to help those who are promoted or transferred to jobs of a different type, which require a different approach.

General management courses should be revised so that they are limited to the provision of information and to the study of problems that are of real value for all job types.

The implications of this research are not confined to industry. The approach, though not the details, can apply in other types of organisation. This is true both of the concept of job types and of the lessons on how to organise one's working-day efficiently, which are discussed in the last chapter.

8 What *Do* Managers Do?

Studies over nearly forty years have changed the traditional picture of what managers do. This chapter tells us what has been learned so far and looks at its implications for the individual manager.

The question 'What does a manager do?' is not an easy one to answer. One can ask what a waiter does and then go and watch him at work. Provided that one has a logical plan for one's observation, one will come back with a clear picture of his job. Observing waiters in other types of restaurants will show some differences but also considerable similarities. It will not be difficult to describe the common core of the job, the scope for individual differences, and how the job differs in different kinds of restaurants. Managers' jobs are both more complicated and far more varied. They differ within the same organisation. Similar jobs in another organisation are likely to differ too. Individual managers also do their jobs very differently so that asking two people in similar jobs to describe what they do is likely to produce at least somewhat different answers. Hence no study can tell us all about what managers do, but only about some aspects. Nor can it tell us all about their jobs since each manager will have his or her idiosyncratic view of, and approach to, the job. The answers to the question posed in the title are important for two reasons:

1. So that all those who can benefit from knowing what managing is really like will not have a mistaken view of it. This includes managers themselves if they are interested in improving their effectiveness, and all those involved in management education and development.
2. To diagnose common ways in which managers may be tempted to act inefficiently.

MAIN CHARACTERISTICS

The reports from the researchers are like those of an anthropologist describing a strange culture: they describe what is distinctive about managers' behaviour. What comes across very strongly from these reports is how different is the reality of the working day from that suggested by the traditional description of a manager as someone who plans, organises, coordinates, motivates and controls. The main characteristics of how managers behave shown by the studies are described below.

Fragmentation

It is the brevity of most activities that is the dominant characteristic of a manager's day at all levels in the hierarchy. Managers switch their attention frequently from one person and one subject to another. The average duration of each episode is measured in minutes as the study in this book, and other studies, show.

Managers typically spend very little time alone and uninterrupted. The 160 managers in this study spent on average only nine such periods of half an hour or longer during the four weeks. A later study showed that the interruptions come not only from other people, but also from the managers themselves, who think of something else and switch to that rather than continuing with their current task.[1]

It's mainly talk

This is the second major characteristic of the manager's day. It is by talking and listening that managers get most of their work done. The amount of time that managers spend with others depends upon the job and its context and upon the individual's inclination. The 160 managers in this study spent two-thirds of their time in conversations. Other studies have found an even higher proportion, probably because of differences in their sample. (The reasons for differences in contact time were discussed on pp. 35–8.) Many managers today have to cope with a faster rate of change than at the time of this study so are likely to have to spend even more time talking and listening. As Horne and Lupton said, in describing their study of sixty-six middle managers in ten companies in different industries in the UK:

> Managers talk most of the time, and mostly face to face. They seem not to be overwhelmed with paper or formal meetings. They swop information and advice and instructions, mostly through informal face to face contact in their own offices.[2]

This comment could equally have been written today rather than more than twenty years ago.

The nature of the contacts differs in different jobs. Chief executives and general managers will often spend a lot of time with people outside the organisation, so will managers at other levels in jobs like sales and purchasing. Many middle managers, and often foremen and junior managers too, have a lot of horizontal contacts. This led Burns, in an early study, to conclude that:

> The accepted view of management as a working hierarchy on organization chart lines may be dangerously misleading. Management simply does not operate as a flow of information up through a succession of filters, and a flow of decisions and instructions down through a succession of amplifiers.[3]

Instead managing is often a political process of getting information and help from, and influencing many, people outside the straight-line hierarchy.

The importance of the boss and subordinates to one's success varies greatly from one job to another. In some it is the cooperation of one's peers that matters more. The time spent with the boss is a crude guide to mutual dependence and to the uncertainty in the relationship. The average time that the 160 managers spent with their boss was 8 per cent but there were great variations as the table on p. 42 shows. Senior managers are often more concerned with relations with their peers and with the outside world than with their subordinates. Indeed in many organisations one notices a divide between the middle management world which is either running or serving the operations, and the top management world whose main concerns and contacts are each other and the external world.

Three other characteristics of much managerial work stem from the two simple observations about fragmentation of the day and the amount of time spent talking. These are discussed under the next three headings: establishing cooperative relationships; using informal information; and managing on the run.

Establishing cooperative relationships

The importance of being able to enlist the support of a diverse range of contacts outside one's own staff is a theme of studies from the 1960s on. Horne and Lupton, for example, commented:

> Middle management does not seem ... to require the exercise of

> remarkable powers to analyse, weigh alternatives and decide. Rather it calls for the ability to shape and utilise the person-to-person channels of communication, to influence, to persuade, to facilitate.[4]

and Sayles that 'The one enduring objective is the effort to build and maintain a predictable, reciprocating system of relationships.'[5] Many years later Kotter, in his study of fifteen general managers in the USA, makes a similar observation though of a more senior group of managers:

> The GMs developed cooperative relationships to and among peers, outsiders, their bosses' bosses, and their subordinates' subordinates. Indeed, they develop relationships with (and sometimes among) any and all people upon whom they felt dependent because of their jobs.[6]

He stresses the special effort given to this 'network building' in the early period in a new job.

Using informal information

Many occupations require the use of formal information obtained from papers, books and prepared presentations. Managing is unusual in the extent to which it has been shown to rely on informal information. Some information comes through the formal provision of reports and scheduled meetings, but much comes from other, often brief, contacts. Mintzberg, who studied five chief executives in the USA and reviewed previous research, gives the best account of the importance of informal information and argues that:

> the manager's advantage lies, not in the documented information that is widely available, and which takes much time to process, but in the current non-documented information transmitted largely by word of mouth . . . managers seem to indicate strong preference for current information, much of which is necessarily unsubstantiated (gossip), and for information on events rather than trends . . . This kind of information, not that carried in formal reports, forms the heart of the manager's information system. The manager develops an understanding of his milieu by piecing together all the scraps of data that he can find.[7]

This generalisation is more applicable to chief executives who must look outside their organisation than to those managers whose job is wholly an internal one. The importance of such informal information is therefore greater in some jobs than in others, but it exists in all.

Managing on the run

Managers need to be able to think while they act, as Weick points out: 'thinking is seldom separated from acting (decisions are not made at specific points in time, they accrete)'[8] This has important implications for managing effectively: the need to have a clear idea of what one is aiming at and an altertness to take up opportunities that arise to pursue one's aims. Many activities can be used for more than one purpose by resourceful managers who remember the major objectives that they wish to pursue. A visit to a conference or attendance at a meeting can provide opportunities to meet people who may be helpful for purposes other than the subject of the conference or meeting.[9]

Managers must rely for much of the time upon their habitual reactions if they are to be able to switch their attention so often from one person and subject to another. This places a great responsibility upon the bosses of junior managers to help them to develop effective habitual ways of thinking and acting. The importance of reviewing one's habitual approach, particularly in times of rapid change, is one of the main arguments for periodic management training.

Many managers develop their own philosophy of managing as a guide to how they should act, as anyone who interviews managers quickly discovers. They also develop guidelines, that is ways of acting, that they have found worked in the past. A manager's philosophy and even more his or her guidelines are tested in a new job. It is then that managers can least rely on habitual ways of thinking and acting, which is why a new job can be exhausting, exhilerating, stressful and a stimulus to learning.

TEMPTATIONS TO INEFFICIENCY

The picture that we now have of how managers spend their time suggests certain temptations to inefficiency that are inherent in their working pattern. Many of these were first noted by Sune Carlson when he was studying managing directors nearly forty years ago. They remain as true today.

Not in control

> Before we made the study, I always thought of a chief executive as the conductor of an orchestra, standing aloof on his platform. Now I am in some respects inclined to see him as a puppet in a puppet-show with hundreds of people pulling the strings and forcing him to act in one way or another.[10]

This was Sune Carlson's all-too-vivid comment on his study of managing directors. He said that they were slaves to their diaries: what they did was what was in their engagement book, and the entries in it were often determined by others. Managers do not see themselves as puppets, but many worry about whether they are sufficiently in control, or indeed know what is going on below them.

Those managers who feel more confident about what is happening in their part of the organisation adopt a planned approach to using their time. They schedule regular meetings with individual subordinates and keep notes of the things to be discussed then. If they believe that visiting their operations is important they schedule this too so that it does not get pushed out by the pressure of other activities. They know what they are trying to do by visiting rather than just doing so as a form of relaxation. They reserve time to devote themselves to the problems that most need their attention.

Superficiality

This is a danger inherent in a fragmented and brief pattern of work. Mintzberg identified it as a prime occupational hazard of the manager. He urged managers to deal consciously with the pressures that encourage a superficial response to problems, in part by delegation, and in part by distinguishing between issues that required special attention.[11] The next chapter will help managers to tackle this problem themselves.

Overworking

Carlson worried about the excessive workload of his managing directors: 'With one exception all the executives we interviewed testified that in the long run they could not continue with their present amount of work' (p. 75) Kotter in his study of general managers also refers to the long hours of those he studied: an average of 59 hours a week. This was not a problem for many of the 160 managers in this study who averaged just over 42 hours a week. Times have changed: more managers below the top also work long hours, but for many there is still some choice.

Mistaken beliefs

Various studies have shown that managers do not know how they spend their time. Also, as Carlson pointed out, they may overrate the time that they spend on some activity which they believe to be important:

> the chief executives themselves regarded personal inspection tours in plants and offices as a most important duty . . . most executives seemed to be mistaken as to the amount of inspection work that they actually did. Wishful thinking led them to believe that things were not so bad as they really were. To the question: 'How often do you make inspection tours in the plant?' we frequently got answers like 'once a fortnight' or 'once every three weeks' in spite of the fact that the executive in question had not been down in the plant for several months.[12]

The same illusion can be found amongst many senior managers today.

A different form of mistaken belief, that is strongly held by some managers, is that everything they do is a demand, that is work that they must do. They fail to recognise that much of what they do reflects their own personal interests and experience. It is in reality a choice that might not be exercised by someone else in the job. The extent of the choice that exists in managerial jobs to do some kinds of work and not others, to emphasise certain aspects of the job and to minimise or ignore others, is itself another characteristic of managerial work – one that also has implications for working effectively.[13] How to deal with some of these temptations to inefficiency is the subject of the next chapter.

9 Too Little Time? How to Help Yourself

This chapter stems from what the managers who kept the research diary learned about how to use their time better. It was their reactions that first interested the author in helping managers to work more effectively and efficiently. This chapter will show you how to find out what you are doing that makes inefficient use of your time. In doing so it draws on the author's long experience of using diaries to help managers to review and improve their use of time.

'Too little time' is the complaint of many managers. They think of this as a fact of life, rather than as amenable to change. They may be like the gardener who thinks of the amount of wind in her garden as a condition that determines what she can grow. She envies her neighbour's wider variety of plants, but does not notice the thought that has gone into providing windbreaks. So managers who analyse their work are like the wise gardener who knows what restrictions of her environment she must accept, but knows also what she can hope to change so as to do more of the things that she wants to do.

When you are very busy and under pressure it is difficult to find the time to take stock of the way you work. Yet the effort is worthwhile. Those who make it usually find that they can organise more effectively both what they do and how they do it. Such an examination must look at both content and organisation. It must aim to answer the two questions: 'Am I doing the right job?' and 'Am I working in the most efficient way?'

It is hard for you as a manager to be certain whether you can say 'Yes' to either question. Fortunately there are danger signals, which if you are alert to them can warn you that something is wrong. One is that there are some aspects of your job that you think are important, but for which you can never find time. Another is a feeling of being constantly under pressure. Many men and women thrive on such a sensation, but in the long run it will lead to inefficiency, and often in the short term too. Yet another danger signal, and the most dangerous of all, is the belief that you are indispensable. It shows either that you have lost your sense of proportion, and had better take a holiday, or that you have failed to select and train your staff properly and to give them sufficient responsibility. Habitual long hours are another warning that you need to change how you work. These danger signals point to bad work organisation. They may also be a sign that you are doing the wrong kind of work. A study of the efficiency of your work must start by looking at the content of what you do.

MAKING THE BEST USE OF ONE'S TIME

Content

Are you doing the right job? You may be very busy, but are you busy on the right things? This is the most important question for you as a manager to ask. It is also one that you, like other managers, are unlikely to have asked. This may be because you think that the answer is self-evident: of course you are doing the right job. It may be because a negative reply would be too uncomfortable. Or, most likely, it is because you are so caught up in the pressure of day-to-day work that you have never stopped to ask the question. Perhaps you have asked, but do not know how to find an answer.

Objectives

An examination of the content of your work must start with job objectives. You may be fortunate and work for a manager who practises a clear performance appraisal based on mutually agreed objectives. Many managers in other organisations are vague about their objectives. They can give a general description of them such as: to make a profit, or in a hospital to provide the best service possible for patients, within the limits of accommodation and medical knowledge. Often, however, they fail to translate these general aims into the detailed objectives that are essential to knowing what one should be doing to achieve them. Let us take staff development as an example of an objective that should be common to all management jobs. Most managers would agree that it is important, but few will have considered what training or development is needed by each of their subordinates or set specific objectives for what should be done to develop them in the next year. Again, most managers would probably agree that one of their objectives should be to cut out unnecessary work, though most are unlikely to include this in any list that they prepare of their objectives. Still less are they likely to spell out the detailed objectives necessary to achieve this aim, such as periodically examining all routine paperwork to ensure that it fulfils a useful purpose.

A consideration of objectives should include an understanding of the time-span of the job. Is it one that requires much attention to future needs? If so, in what areas and how far ahead should you be planning? In addition to planning for their own function, most managers should think about future staffing needs and the development of their staff. Of all long-term objectives, plans for staff development are most likely to be continually postponed under the pressure of more immediate problems.

Once the objectives have been defined in detail, you should ask yourself how far you have fulfilled them in the past six months. Your answer, if it is to be adequate, cannot be given off the cuff. Some discrepancies between objectives and practice may be evident from thinking about what you have done in the past six months, but others will only be shown up by an analysis of what you are doing from day to day.

There are three common ways in which managers may fail to pursue the right objectives. The first is by neglecting longer-term objectives because of the thousands of day-to-day matters that need attention. The second is by an unbalanced division of time between objectives. Luijk, in a study of twenty-five Dutch directors, concluded that twenty-one of them divided their time inadequately between the different areas of the business. They spent too much time on their favourite areas and too little on those that interested them less.[1] The third common reason for not pursuing the right objectives is a failure to realise when objectives need modifying because of changes in the nature of the job. Sune Carlson's study of nine managing directors showed that some of them tended to discount as abnormal activities that had continued for so long that they should have been treated as part of the normal job.[2] One of the dangerous advantages of labelling something as abnormal is that one need not rethink and replan one's work to make time for it.

What happens in practice

It is often salutary to compare what you think you do with what happens in practice. Managers who do this often find quite a difference. To check, you must keep a record of how you actually spend your time. It is usually best to start by keeping a general record for at least a week of everything that you do, choosing a week that is fairly typical, if you are in a job that has such weeks! If not, you should try to keep a record for longer, or of sample periods at different times. A suitable record form is given below. It needs to be kept as far as possible as you go along, NOT filled in by memory. There is a column marked 'fleeting contacts' for very brief conversations that you do not have time to record more fully. Keeping this diary may alert you to some aspects of the way you work that surprise and disturb you. More can be learned by using the following list of questions to check whether you are content with what you are doing and how you do it:

1. Am I giving adequate attention to current activities, to reviewing the past and to planning for the future? In particular, am I giving enough thought to the future?
2. Am I dividing my time correctly between different aspects of my job? Is there, perhaps, one part of my job on which I spend too much of my time?
3. Have I changed what I am trying to do, and how I work, to allow for the effects of changes in my work?
4. Am I doing work that I ought to have delegated?
5. Who are the people that I ought to be seeing? Am I spending too much or too little time with any of them?
6. Do I organise my working day and week, as far as possible, according to priorities, or do I tend to deal with each problem as it turns up, or even as I think of it, without stopping to consider whether there is something more important that I should be working on?
7. Am I able to complete a task, or am I constantly interrupted? If the latter, are all these interruptions an essential part of my work?

A check through your record of time spent should show whether you can answer 'yes' to question 1. A common failing is spending too much time on short-term tasks. Unless you give a clear 'yes' to question 1, it is worth listing your longer-term objectives, and asking what you have done during the past year to further each of them.

If you are doubtful whether you can say 'Yes' to questions 2 or 4, look at your time record to see if it is all work that you should be doing. Check this by asking three questions of each of your activities.

DIARY 1
General Record

DAY	TIME	BRIEF DESCRIPTION		CONTACTS							
			Alone	Tel.	Face to face	Subs	Boss	Other Internal to the Divison/ Subsidiary	Other Parts of the Parent Company	Ext. to the Company	Change of Activity

Should it be done at all? If so, when should it be done? Should it be delegated? You may be doing work that you carried over from the previous job, which should now be done by your successor. You may be doing work that could be done more easily and more efficiently with the help of specialist advice. Most frequently, managers find that some of their work ought to be delegated. Ten of the managers taking part in the research decided after keeping the diary that they should streamline routine work and delegate more. As one of them said, 'Keeping the diary was salutary: it highlighted the time spent on work that should be done by subordinates.'

The rest of this chapter contains illustrations of different kinds of diaries that you can use to check on specific aspects of the content or organisation of your work. Which can help you will depend upon how satisfied you are with your answers to the questions above. Before reading the text you may find it helpful to scan the range of diaries that are illustrated.

One way in which you can check the content of your work is to keep a record for some weeks of all the subjects with which you are concerned, and how you came to be involved in them. For each subject you should ask three questions: (i) did I need to be concerned with it at all?; (ii) did I need to be concerned at that stage?; and (iii)

DIARY 2

Analysis of Content of Work

(1) Brief description of subject	(2) How was I involved? By							(3) Did I need to be concerned		
	Self	Boss	Subordinates	Colleagues	Customers	Others		At all?	At that stage?	In so much detail?

did I need to be involved in so much detail? A record sheet for such an analysis might look like Diary 2. In column 3 put a tick for Yes or a cross for No. Adapt the divisions in section 2 to suit your own job. If you are putting some crosses in section 3, section 2 will help you to trace the cause, so will section 1. You should also look at your completed diary to see whether there are parts of the work that seem to recur too often or too seldom. If there are, keep a note for as long as necessary of the amount of time that you spend working on that part of your job.

To answer question 3, first ask yourself whether there have been any major recent changes in the job, then look at your diary 2 to see whether they are adequately reflected in what you are doing.

Managers may be able to save more time by efficiently organising their discussions with other people than in any other way. The research findings underlined the truth of the statement that managers work with other people. The average amount of time that the 160 managers spent in discussions with other people was 66 per cent, but today most managers spend even more time. Is this high proportion of the working day well spent? To answer this – that is, question 5 on the check list – you should know who are the people you should be seeing and how much time you should normally need to spend with them.

When you have a visitor your secretary should know in what circumstances you are to be interrupted, but should otherwise ensure that the conversation is undisturbed. Your visitor should never need to resort to the strategy reported in a story, which may be apocryphal, of a visit by Keynes to Roosevelt, which was interrupted by frequent telephone calls. After some time Keynes left the room and telephoned Roosevelt, who expressed surprise. Keynes replied, 'I realise that the telephone is the only way to get your attention'.

Decide what your contact pattern should be. To do this well is more difficult than it may appear because you should think hard about what are the real reasons why you need to see different people. Your subordinates, for example, may be both competent and well motivated. The main reason for seeing them may be to exchange information. Now check to see how far your actual pattern accords with what you think it should be. Look at the first diary that you kept to see if it gives you enough information. If not, and it raises doubts in your mind about how you distribute your time between different people, then you could benefit from keeping a specific record of your contacts as illustrated in Diary 3.

DIARY 3
Analysis of Contacts

Column 1 *Length of time*	Column 2 *Persons contacted*	Column 3 *Brief description of topic*

Recording should be by a tick in the appropriate column in section 1. Section 2 should have subdivisions for each of your main contacts; other contacts should be grouped under appropriate headings. Section 2 should be filled in by a tick if you saw the person alone and a cross if anybody else was present, or both if you did both. If you did not keep Diary 2, you might add the third column of that diary to the Contacts Diary, so as to be able to judge more easily how many of your discussions were necessary.

The contact time over which one has most control is that spent with subordinates. It is also much the most time-consuming part of a manager's contacts – an average of 26 per cent of the time of managers taking part in the research – so that good use of this time is particularly important. In checking the efficiency of your discussions with subordinates, look at both the topics discussed and the time that you spent with each subordinate. If you kept Diary 2, the Analysis of Content of Work, you may already have spotted weaknesses in delegation. If you did not keep Diary 2 but added its last column to the Contacts Diary, it will help you to diagnose your weaknesses in delegation.

The diary may show that you spent a great deal of time with one or two subordinates. Is this desirable? There may have been good reasons for it, such as a particular problem affecting the work of one subordinate or the need to give more guidance to a subordinate who was new to the job. An analysis of the diary may, however, show no good reason. Then you should ask whether the fault is yours or the subordinate's or both. The explanation may be that this subordinate works in your favourite area and is, therefore, more often called in to discuss it. If so, is this using time efficiently and is it being fair to the subordinate? Another reason may be that you enjoy this subordinate's company. If so, you should consider the repercussions on other staff. Yet another reason may be that the subordinate is reluctant to make decisions and so comes too often to ask for advice or confirmation.

The diary may also show that you spent very little time with one subordinate and almost never saw him or her alone. Again ask yourself whether this is satisfactory. The subordinate may be in such command of the job that you rarely need to discuss it, but there can be other less desirable explanations. You may not like him or her and so may try to avoid contact, or you may not be as interested as you should be in the problems with which the subordinate has to deal.

Other kinds of contacts will be important in particular jobs; in some it will be customers, in others colleagues, in yet others, people in similar jobs in other companies. You can easily see from the diary whether you seem to be spending too much or too little time with one individual or one class of contact and should then ask yourself why this is. You may like to compare the distribution of your contact time with that of the managers in the research, asking yourself why you are unusual, if you are. Is is the nature of your job or the way that you do it? Indeed, the record of how you divide your time between different types of contact can tell you a lot about the kind of job you are doing. Some managers spend most of their time with their subordinates. Others give more time to contacts with their boss, managers in other departments, or with people outside the organisation. Most jobs offer you choices as to where you place your emphasis: downwards, sideways, upwards or outwards. Look at your Contacts Diary to see which you are doing and ask yourself whether that fits with what you are trying to accomplish in the job.

In some jobs, your place of work can offer another guide to whether you are fulfilling your objectives. If, for example, you aim to spend a certain proportion of the working week visiting customers, inspecting the works, or going to subsidiary companies, a record for some weeks of where you are can be a simple check of how far you are achieving this objective.

Organising your work

Once you are satisfied that the content of your work is right, turn to the way you work and ask yourself whether you can improve that. Can you give a satisfactory answer to question 6 of the check list? You may reply, as some managers do, that the question does not concern you because the nature of the job makes it impossible for you to try to organise your time. You may resent any suggestion that you could improve the organisation of your own work. Yet an essential feature of the jobs of all managers who have subordinates is organising the work of others. It seems unlikely that your job cannot be organised. First, ask yourself whether the time with subordinates is organised efficiently. There are two opposing dangers for the boss: being too readily available or too inaccessible. The former is bad for the efficient organisation of your work, the latter is frustrating for your subordinates. One of the lessons drawn by some of the managers who kept the diary was the need to organise the time when their subordinates could see them, establishing regular discussions for which they prepared and encouraged their subordinates to do so too. Additionally, some of the managers decided that to help with unexpected problems it was inefficient to say 'My door is open.' One should say instead 'My door is open between 2.30 and 3.30. If you want to come then let me know so that you do not need to wait. Come at other times only if the problem needs immediate attention.' There may be jobs where the manager needs always to be available to subordinates, but they are the minority. Most managers are not, and should not be, as indispensable as that.

Too-frequent interruptions by subordinates can disorganise the manager's work, but the boss can also hamper the work of subordinates. You should remember that subordinates also have their own work to do and that you should try not to disturb them every time you think of something, but keep a folder of points to be raised at your regular meetings. Some managers need to check whether they are available enough. Your secretary could keep a record of who has been trying to talk to you and how long it was before they were able to do so. Then try to assess the effects of such delays on the work, and possibly on the attitude, of the individuals concerned.

One of the main lessons drawn by many of the managers who took part in the research was the need to work more methodically by deciding work priorities and trying to complete one job before starting another. 'I tried to cut down self-inflicted interruptions' said one manager who realised while keeping the research diary that many of the interruptions to his work, about which he had previously complained, were self-imposed. Some of the managers were appalled at the unorganised nature of their working day – this was brought home to them when they had to make a fresh diary entry for each change in activity. 'I found that keeping a diary reduced the "grasshopping" tendency to jump from topic to topic' said another manager. Some also found that keeping a visible record encouraged some of their callers to be briefer than usual!

Fragmentation

The reasons for unnecessary fragmentation of the working day may be your method of working, or other people's. It is hard to admit to oneself that a fragmented day is often the laziest day; the day that demands the least in terms of mental discipline, though the most in nervous energy. It is easier to pass from one subject to a second when the first requires a difficult or unpalatable decision, or sustained thought. It is easier to respond to each fresh stimulus, to hare after the latest query, than to set an order of priorities and try to keep to it. This, of course, includes knowing when the latest query has priority. It is easier to be a grasshopper jumping from one problem to another, than a beaver chewing away at a tough task.

A simple way to check whether you have grasshopper tendencies that are not entirely imposed by the nature of your job is to keep each day for a week a consecutive list of all the activities with which you are concerned. The list should repeat an item if there has been a break in that activity. The analysis sheet for this kind of check might look like Diary 4. Columns 3 and 4 can be filled in by ticks. If there are a lot of ticks in 3b and 4d these show the need to plan your priorities and to be strict with yourself in keeping to them. You may be the kind of person who enjoys jumping from one thing to another, rather than persevering with one at a time. If there are a lot of ticks in 4c it shows that you need to examine your contacts with other people – questions 5 and 7 of the check list. How you might do so has already been discussed.

You may want to tick 4b because you decided to put a problem or a difficult report on one side and come back to it. This can be a productive break because we all know, and should make use of the fact, that some of our thinking and problem resolution takes place without conscious effort. So it is often a good idea to do some preliminary work and return to the problem later.

If you think that you have a lot of interruptions (Question 7) first check your fleeting contacts of under five minutes. The record from diary 1 or from the Contacts Diary may have alerted you to a problem. If so, you may think it worth using Diary 5 to get more information

DIARY 4

Work Priorities Diary

Column 1 *Time*	Column 2 *Brief description of activity*	Column 3 *Was this something I should have been doing then?*		Column 4 *Reason for stopping*			
		(a) Yes	(b) No	(a) Finished	(b) Unfinished but necessary	(c) Unnecessary Caused by others	(d) Unnecessary Caused by self

about the causes. Column 1 will be filled in by ticks. Column 2 may be subdivided with a division for each of your main contacts, or groups of contacts, so that it too can be filled in by ticks. Column 4 should just have a tick if it was an interruption, that is, a brief conversation that took place when you were working on a different subject. It may be an interruption, even if you initiated it.

DIARY 5

Analysis of Fleeting Contacts

Column 1 *Type of contact*		Column 2 *Who was it with?*	Column 3 *Who initiated it?*		Column 4 *Was it an interruption?*
Personal	Telephone		Self	Other	

You should compare the number of your fleeting contacts with those of the managers who took part in the research shown in Figure 6.5, taking as a comparison the number for the group that you think you would be in. Even if your total is about the same, you may still, like some of the 160 managers, want to change your habits. One of them said he found that keeping the diary was 'Frightening. I am trying to cut down the number of interruptions.' This has been a comment over the years of many managers after keeping a record of how they spent their time.

Some managers will naturally have more interruptions than others, both fleeting and longer contacts, as they will need to be more readily available to subordinates, colleagues or customers. Your job may require you to be interrupted frequently, if your function is to deal with other people's queries and problems. However, once you have kept a record of fleeting contacts you may find that some of the interruptions are self-created, and that others are due to poor organisation of your work, to inadequate delegation or to encouraging or permitting people who do not need to do so to come to you at any time.

It will be hardest to reduce the interruptions that are caused by your boss. You should try to educate him not to call you whenever he thinks of it. A good approach might be to tell him that you are trying to organise your work more efficiently, so that you will have clear periods to work on certain problems – choose as an example a topic in which the boss is particularly interested. Ask him what is the most convenient time for you to talk with him.

Clarity and brevity

Talking and listening are the most time-consuming parts of managers' jobs, but doing so can easily be a waste of your own and other people's time. Woolly thinking or verbosity on either side can double the time taken to discuss or explain something. If you are prone to either – and often they are related – practise writing a report as shortly and clearly as you can. If you examine what you write, or, better still, can get someone else to do so, you may find that much of it is rambling and confused and can be expressed more clearly and concisely. You need to be able to think clearly and to express yourself well, and to try to train your subordinates to do so too. Practice and criticisms by others will bring improvement.

Too much brevity may offend, but few people err that way. It is worth learning the skill of keeping conversations to the point, when this seems desirable, and of how to bring them to an end. Look for a good example of a manager who wastes no time, but does not cause offence, and study his or her technique. There is the related question of whether you need to spend time on preliminary pleasantries. The extent to which it is acceptable to begin with the topic that is the reason for the meeting varies from country to country. In some, cultural tradition still demands lengthy preliminaries before the purpose of the meeting can be mentioned. In Britain and the USA a more direct approach is acceptable. Since such preliminaries take up a lot of time, look critically if you indulge in ritual small talk and ask whether it really improves relations. Sometimes such talk can become merely a habit, so that the other person is only too well aware that you are uninterested in replies to questions about the family's health.

One general manager said that he had increased his output by about 15 per cent as a result of keeping the diary. He spent less time gossiping and generally became more conscious of the time he wasted. It is, he said, 'so easy to lose five minutes between jobs'.

Travelling

An often neglected aspect of the efficient use of time is attention to the time lost in travelling. For a third of the managers taking part in the research, travelling, other than to and from their home, took up more than 10 per cent of their working day. For many, probably for all those who drove themselves and for many who went by public transport, this was lost time. Travelling is such a large potential time-waster that it must be carefully planned. Before going ask: Is this trip necessary? Why? On return repeat the questions. The means of travel is also relevant. Driving is often the most tiring form of transport. If the journey is by train or plane, use for work the time that you do not need for relaxation. A long journey provides the opportunity for thinking through a problem, away from the distractions and interruptions of office life.

Body-rhythms

We are all more capable of concentration and more sociable at some time of day than at others. Though, as married couples often find out, these rhythms are not the same for everybody. It is worth planning the timing of different activities to take account of your natural ups and downs.

Thinking

A more difficult type of analysis than any of those that have been suggested is that of one's reactions to problems. There are two dangers to be avoided. One is to react too impulsively to problems that need thought. The other is to react in a stereotyped way when it is inappropriate. Many managers put a premium on quick reactions and never stop to examine whether their reactions are still the right ones. 'Speed is of the essence' is a saying that many accept without question, but speed can be very expensive if it means skipping an essential planning stage. Many managers shirk the task of examining the reasons for failures or for only partial success. Such an examination may show that some of the necessary planning was not done because of the enthusiasm to get on with the project.

Individuals and groups develop habitual responses as a means of economising time and energy. One of management's objectives should be to ensure that these responses and ways of approaching problems do not get out of date. In the rapidly changing environment in which many organisations have to operate, managers should do all they can to avoid becoming mentally set. Ask yourself how long it is since you thought of dealing with a particular kind of problem in a different way. Your subordinates, especially if they are younger and have been in the company a shorter time than you have may be better able to criticise existing methods and approaches. Research workers or consultants should also be able to help you to look at your problems afresh; just by asking questions they may show you a different approach to your work.

Developing

Most development comes on the job. You may have been fortunate and had jobs which stretched and challenged you in different ways. Even so, you will learn more if you try to reflect on your experiences. In thinking about your use of time you should ask what you have done recently to further your own development. How long is it since you read a book or article related to your work? Do you try to expose yourself to people who will challenge your thinking and behaviour? When did you last do so?

DO YOU REALLY WANT MORE TIME?

'Too little time' is the most respectable reason for neglecting some aspect of one's job, but it is rarely a sufficient explanation. It is your job, as a manager, to try to organise your work and that of your subordinates so that you do have time. Unfortunately, in too many companies it is respectable to be busy and to work long hours; a manager with a clear desk and time to think would be regarded with suspicion. Few people, however, incur such suspicion for it is easier to be busy than not. Parkinson's Law remains true – 'that work expands to fill the time available'.[3]

If you complain that you have no time, ask yourself whether you really regret this. You may be happiest when you are at the centre of activity, necessary or not. You may love bustle, people coming to you for information and decisions. You may enjoy showing your power in coping with crises, unaware of the fact that with more care they could have been avoided. You may be glad when people say that they want to speak to you, instead of ensuring that as many callers as possible are dealt with by your subordinates. You may pride yourself on being indispensable. Indeed the last thing that you may want to have is more time. Time to worry – no! Merciful busyness will protect you from that.

In conclusion, if you are to do the right work and to do it efficiently, certain things are necessary. First and foremost, to define your objectives; next, to give sufficient time to pursuing each of them. Immediate demands should not be satisfied at the expense of long-term aims or one aspect of the job receive too much attention unless there is a good reason for doing so. Few managers will have sufficient time unless they know how to delegate. You should have taught your subordinates what they can do without referene to you, what things you need to know, when the subordinates should consult you, and at what times you are available for normal discussion. Finally, most managers have to train themselves to organise their work; that is, to do the jobs that they should do, rather than the ones they like, are familiar with or find easiest, and to resist the temptation to jump impulsively from one thing to another.

One of the barriers to organising one's work effectively is the belief that one is indispensable. This is a reassuring fallacy to the manager who is afraid of not being needed; to the extent that it is true, it is a sign of poor management.

Appendices

Appendix I The Diary used in the Research

FOR EPISODES LASTING 5 MINUTES OR MORE

Please start a fresh sheet whenever there is a change under any one of the headings: 'Did you do this', 'Where?', 'Who?', 'How?', 'What?'. This means that, except for 'Who?', there should never be more than one tick under one of these headings.

* 'Incident' is what you have taken a fresh sheet to record, that is a change in one of the headings.

a. 'Other units' means other establishments, divisions, or subsidiary companies belonging to the same parent company.

b. 'Colleagues' are those reporting to the same line boss as you.

c. 'Fellow Specialists' are those doing a similar job to you, in another department, or elsewhere in the parent company. They may or may not be at the same level as you.

d. 'Committee' is any pre-arranged group meeting. It may or may not have an agenda.

e. 'Discussion' is talking, which is not classified under one of the other headings.

f. 'Social' is when work is combined with a social activity.

g. 'Writing & Co. reading' includes dealing with correspondence. Company reading is of material produced by the company.

h. 'Other work' means just thinking. But please read more detailed notes.

i. 'Inspection' is a personal tour of work place.

j. 'Travelling' is when you are travelling for your work and *not* doing any other work listed under 'How?'.

k. 'General management' is when you are dealing with two or more management functions, such as sales and production, at the same time, or in the same meeting. But if there is a clear division between the discussions on two functions, please record on separate sheets.

For more detailed information about headings, please see separate instructions.

FOR CONTACTS OF UNDER 5 MINUTES

Please enter in Fleeting Contacts section below.

There may be a number of such fleeting contacts during the main incident that you have recorded above, or before you start a fresh sheet. So you can have a number of ticks in this section.

When recording a fleeting contact no entries should be made in the main section of the diary, but a tick should be put in the adjoining column if this interrupts what you were doing.

Time of Starting Incident?*......................

Duration: Hrs..................... Mins..................... (nearest 5 mins.)

DID YOU DO THIS							
Alone?[0]............		With one other person?[1]....		With 2 or more?[2]............			
WHERE?		WHO?		HOW?		WHAT?	
0	Own Office	+	INTERNAL Boss	+	Committees[d]	0	Finance
1	Other internal	–	Boss's boss	–	Discussions[e]	1	General management[k]
2	Other units[a]	0	Secretary	0	Selection interviewing	2	Marketing and Sales
3	External	1	Subordinates	1	Social[f]	3	Personnel
4	Home	2	Subordinates' subordinates	2	Telephoning	4	Production
5	Travelling	3	Colleagues[b]	3	Figure work	5	Public Relations
		4	Fellow[c] Specialists	4	Reading, external	6	Purchasing
		5	Other internal	5	Writing & Co. reading[g]	7	Research and Development
		6	Other units[a]	6	Other work[h]	8	
		7	EXTERNAL Customers	7	Inspection[i]		
		8	Suppliers	8	Lectures and conferences		
		9	Other external	9	Travelling[j]		

FLEETING CONTACTS

	Personal	Telephone	Interruption?
Boss	0	0	0
Secretary	1	1	1
Subordinates	2	2	2
Other internal Other units	3	3	3
External	4	4	4

Appendix II

Analysis of the Sample

The information in the following tables was obtained from the background questionnaires completed by each manager. Tables 1 to 5 give factual information about the company for which the manager worked. Table 6 gives the number of subordinates reporting directly to the manager and Table 7 his total number of subordinates.

Table 1 *Industrial groups*

Industry	*No. in sample*	*% Total sample*	*Distribution of manufacturing industries* Sample %	Nat. av. %[1]
Manufacturing Industries				
1. Food, Drink and Tobacco	13	8.2	9.1	9.1
2. Chemicals and Allied Industries	32	20.0	22.4	5.9
3. Metal Manufacture	4	2.5	2.8	7.1
4. Engineering and Electrical Goods	41	25.6	28.6	26.1
5. Shipbuilding and Marine Engineering	..	..	..	2.2
6. Vehicles	9	5.6	6.3	9.7
7. Other Metal Goods	25	15.6	17.5	6.7
8. Textiles	4	2.5	2.8	8.6
9. Leather, Leather Goods and Fur	..	..	..	0.7
10. Clothing and Footwear	1	0.6	0.7	6.0
11. Bricks, Pottery, Glass, Cement, etc.	..	..	..	3.9
12. Timber, Furniture, etc.	1	0.6	0.7	3.3
13. Paper, Printing and Publishing	12	7.5	8.4	7.0
14. Other	1	0.6	0.7	3.7
TOTAL: All Manufacturing Industries	(143)	(89.3)	100.0	100.0
Other Industries				
15. Gas, Electricity and Water	14	8.8		
16. Distributive Trades	1	0.6		
17. Miscellaneous Services	2	1.3		
TOTAL: Other Industries	(17)	(10.7)		
TOTAL: Whole Sample	160	100.0		

[1]Based on Employment Figures for Jan. 1966 (*Ministry of Labour Gazette*, Mar. 1966).

*Table 2 Numbers employed in UK**

	Total
11–99	7
100–249	8
250–499	16
500–999	14
1000–1999	12
2000–4999	12
5000 +	90
No information	1

Table 3 Numbers employed in the establishment where the manager worked

	Total
11–99	32
100–249	28
250–499	32
500–999	20
1000–1999	24
2000–4999	15
5000 +	9

Table 4 Method of production

	Total
Process	29
Mass	19
Batch	39
One-off	8
Batch/One-off	16
All	5
Process/Mass/Batch	3
Mass/Batch/One-off	2
Batch/Process	5
Mass/Batch	7
Mass/Process	1
Mass/One-off	2
No information	24

Table 5 Areas in which the managers worked

	Total
London and South-East	72
Eastern	5
Southern	7
South-West	3
Midland	20
North Midland	7
East and West Ridings	10
North-West	4
North	24
Scotland	5
Wales	2
Ireland and Overseas	1

Table 6 Number of immediate subordinates

	Total
1–3	26
4–6	54
7–9	36
10–11	11
12 +	28
None	3
No information	2

Table 7 Total number of subordinates

	Total
1–10	19
11–49	42
50–99	27
100–250	32
251–500	19
501–999	10
1000 +	8
None	2
No information	1

*Figures are for the parent company, if any.

Appendix III

Details of the Individual Managers, divided into Five Groups

Job	Level[1]	Numbers controlled: No. of immediate subordinates	No. of subordinates' subordinates	Type of company: Industry[2]	Number of employees in the UK[3]	in subsidiary[4]
GROUP 1. Number 45						
Marketing and Sales						
Sales Director	Top	6	70	Printing	M	..
,,	,,	25	..	Electronics	S	..
Sales Manager	,,	23	500	Engineering	L	M
,,	,,	3	48	,,	M	..
,,	,,	14	30	Heavy engineering	M	..
,,	,,	15	130	Paper and board	L	M/L
,,	,,	8	40	Engineering	L	M
,,	,,	8	150	Electronics	L	..
,,	,,	4	8	Textiles	M/L	..
,,	,,	15	..	Engineering	S	..
,,	,,	7	30	,,	S	..
,,	Middle	5	88	Heavy engineering	M	..

[1]Top managers are those who are on the board of directors or who report to the managing director. Middle managers are those below that level who have other managers or highly paid specialists reporting to them, or who are graded as middle management by their companies. Some of those described as middle managers in large companies have bigger jobs than some of those described as top managers who are in small companies.

[2]'Engineering' is used to describe the industry when a more specific description of the section of the engineering industry concerned might not be sufficiently anonymous.

[3]S (small) = under 250 employees; M (medium) = 250–999 employees; M/L (medium/large) = 1000–4999 employees; L (large) = 5000 plus.

[4]Where the manager works for a subsidiary company, the number of its employees is indicated in this column.

Job	Level[1]	Numbers controlled: No. of immediate subordinates	No. of subordinates' subordinates	Type of company: Industry[2]	Number of employees in the UK[3]	in subsidiary[4]
Sales Manager	Middle	24	122	Agricultural equipment	M	S
,,	,,	6	35	Pharmaceutical	S	..
,,	,,	3	17	Electronics	M/L	M
,,	,,	5	74	Packaging	L	M/L
,,	,,	10	..	Cosmetics	M	L
,,	,,	6	..	Pharmaceutical	L	..
,,	,,	8	..	Cosmetics	M	.L
,,	,,	9	..	,,	M	L
Sales Administration Manager	,,	7	65	Confectionery	L	..
Distribution Manager	,,	7	124	Food	L	M/L
Manager	,,	9	90	,,	L	M/L
Marketing Manager (no selling)	,,	3	18	Engineering	L	..
,,	,,	3	..	Furniture	M	..
,,	Top	1	4	Metal goods	M	..
Marketing Director	,,	7	..	Advertising agency	S	..
General Management						
Sales Director and Joint General Manager	Top	6	180	Scientific instruments	M/L	..
Director	,,	6	1,200	Electronics	L	..
General Manager	,,	50	3,000	Food	L	M/L
,,	,,	6	200	Paper and board	M/L	S
Managing Director	,,	6	45	Consultant engineers	S	..
,,	,,	6	300	Engineering	M	..
Director	,,	7	50	Management consultants	S	..
Director and General Manager	,,	9	467	Chemical	M	..
Joint Managing Director	,,	8	350	Metal goods	M/L	M
Director Production Sales	,,	3	220	Chemical	M	..
Other Managers						
Credit Manager	Middle	2	10	Engineering	L	..
Group Works Manager	Top	8	550	Metal manuf.	M/L	..
Works and Purchasing Manager	Middle	7	700	Food	L	M

Job	Level[1]	Numbers controlled: No. of immediate subordinates	No. of subordinates' subordinates	Type of company: Industry[2]	Number of employees in the UK[3]	in subsidiary[4]
Technical Services Manager	Middle	?	300	Electronics	L	..
Senior Engineer	,,	6	..	Public service	L	..
Civil Engineer	,,	3	55	,,	L	..
,,	,,	7	10	Civil engineering	S	..
Chief Accountant	Top	3	150	Motor	L	..
GROUP 2. Number 33						
Research and Development						
Section Head Computing	Middle	6	..	Public service	L	..
Head Office Engineer	,,	1	..	,,	L	..
Civil Engineer	,,	1	..	,,	L	..
Senior Engineer	,,	9	..	,,	L	..
Section Head	,,	3	10	Paper and board	M	L
Standards Engineer	,,	2	..	Steel	L	..
Other Managers Production and Engineering						
Deputy Chief Engineer	,,	10	16	Paper and board	M	L
Production Manager	,,	6	490	Pharmaceutical	L	M/L
Works Manager	,,	9	95	Chemical	L	S
Production Manager	,,	10	300	Food	L	M
Technical Director	Top	16	..	Chemical	S	..
Production Manager	Middle	2	141	,,	L	..
Works Manager	,,	6	1,500	,,	L	..
Foreman	Junior	12	..	Electronics	L	..
Production Manager	Middle	6	60	Heavy engineering	M	..
Accounting and Secretarial						
Chief Accountant	Top	16	..	Engineering	M/L	S
,,	,,	8	23	Heavy engineering	M	..
Assistant Company Secretary	Middle	4	20	Textiles	L	M
Divisional Accountant	Middle	11	600	Public service	L	..
Section Head Budgetary Control	,,	8	..	Chemical	L	..

Job	Level[1]	Numbers controlled: No. of immediate subordinates	No. of subordinates' subordinates	Type of company: Industry[2]	Number of employees in the UK[3]	in subsidiary[4]
Deputy Company Secretary	Middle	3	9	Electronics	L	..
Chief Accountant	Top	5	22	Light engineering	M	..
,,	,,	30	..	Printing	M	..
Company Secretary	,,	4	16	,,	M	..
Payroll Manager	Middle	4	58	Engineering	L	..
Sales						
Commercial Manager	,,	18	40	Domestic appliances	M/L	..
Sales Manager	,,	6	30	Engineering (mainly overseas sales)	M	..
Sales and Service	Top	13	..	Engineering	S	..
Distribution Manager	Middle	11	180	Food	L	..
Sales Support	,,	4	600	Electronics	L	..
Other						
Managing Director	Top	12 plus agents	..	Merchanting	S	..
Manager, Machine Servicing Department	Middle	15	160	Public service	L	..
General Manager and Company Secretary	Top	4	210	Engineering	S	..
GROUP 3. Number 35						
Accounting and Secretarial						
Assistant Secretary	Middle	7	182	Engineering	L	..
Office Services	,,	7	91	,,	L	..
Chief Accountant	Top	4	101	Paper and board	L	M/L
Office Manager	Middle	5	20	Chemical	L	M
Administration Manager	,,	30	..	Food	L	M
Company Secretary	Top	7	125	Chemical	L	..
Financial Director	Top	4	120	Chemical	L	M/L
Assistant Accountant	Middle	3	24	,,	L	..
Company Secretary	Top	5	45	Electronics	L	..
Assistant Financial Controller	Middle	?	?	,,	L	..
Cost Accountant	,,	3	92	Motor	L	..
Personnel and Training						
Personnel Manager	,,	9	200	Engineering	L	..

Job	Level[1]	Numbers controlled: No. of immediate subordinates	No. of subordinates' subordinates	Type of company: Industry[2]	Number of employees in the UK[3]	in subsidiary[4]
Assistant Training Manager	Middle	1	16 part-time	Steel	L	..
Recruitment Manager	,,	7	12	Electronics	L	..
Personnel Manager	,,	25	..	,,	L	..
Production Control and other production staff						
Superintendent Production Control	,,	9	200	Engineering	L	..
Chief Inspector	,,	2	25	Motor	L	M
Instrument Engineer	,,	4	24	Public service	L	..
Planning and Efficiency Engineer	,,	2	10	,,	L	..
Works Engineer	,,	3	40	Pharmaceutical	M/L	M
Manager Production Engineer	,,	4	95	Heavy engineering	L	..
Manager Central Production Control	,,	4	60	Domestic appliances	L	M/L
Production Controller at Head Office	,,	4	..	Electronics	L	..
Assistant Chief Production Engineer	,,	4	40	Engineering	L	..
Marketing and Sales						
Homes Sales Manager	Top	4	67	Engineering	L	L
Sales Manager	Middle	12	40	Communications	M	L
Sales Manager	Top	6	60	Textiles	M	..
Marketing Director	,,	55	55	Pharmaceutical	L	S
Sales Director	,,	10	200	Rubber	M	..
Other						
Transport Manager	Middle	25	134	Paper and board	L	M
Merchandise Manager	,,	1	..	Retailing	L	M
Division Manager and Personnel Director	Top	10	350	Electrical	M	..
Works Manager	,,	4	290	,,	L	M
Manager of a Development Group	Middle	6	40	Electronics	L	..
Public Relations Officer	,,	4	6	,,	L	..

Job	*Level*[1]	*Numbers controlled*		*Type of company*		
		No. of immediate subordinates	*No. of subordinates' subordinates*	*Industry*[2]	*Number of employees in the UK*[3]	*Number of employees in subsidiary*[4]
GROUP 4. Number 33						
Works and Production Managers						
Deputy Works Manager	Middle	11	183	Public service	L	..
,,	,,	?	158	,,	L	..
,,	,,	8	130	,,	L	..
Factory Manager	,,	6	720	Metal goods	L	..
,,	,,	8	675	,,	L	..
Works Manager	,,	7	900	,,	L	..
Factory Manager	,,	7	300	Textiles	L	M
Works Manager	Top	7	240	Electrical	M	..
,,	Middle	8	260	,,	M	..
Brewer in charge	,,	7	100	Brewing	M/L	..
Soap Plant Manager	,,	6	350	Soap and detergent	L	M/L
Works Manager	Top	13	275	Metal goods	M	..
,,	,,	5	100	Engineering	S	..
,,	Middle	8	950	Food	L	M/L
,,	,,	25	1,700	Chemical	L	..
,,	Top	7	393	Printing	M	..
,,	,,	18	133	Machine tools	S	..
,,	Middle	4	80	Chemicals	M	..
Works Manager	Top	7	350	Chemicals	L	M
Engineering Managers						
Civil Engineer	Middle	4	71	Public service	L	..
,,	,,	6	48	,,	L	..
,,	,,	10	..	,,	L	..
Maintenance Engineer	,,	4	120	,,	L	..
Chief Engineer	,,	5	30	Paper and board	M/L	L
Plant Engineer	,,	19	35	Electrical	L	..
Senior Works Engineer	,,	30	200	Motor	L	..
Engineering Manager	Top	5	40	Medical supplies	M	..
Research and Development						
Chief, new Development Department	,,	18	..	Electronics	L	L
General Management						
General Manager (in charge of one manufacturing unit)	Middle	17	1,260	Metal goods	L	..

Job	Level[1]	Numbers controlled: No. of immediate subordinates	Numbers controlled: No. of subordinates' subordinates	Type of company: Industry[2]	Type of company: Number of employees in the UK[3]	Type of company: Number of employees in subsidiary[4]
Chief Executive (in charge of one manufacturing unit)	Top	4	250	Food	L	M
General Manager	,,	3	74	Motor components	S	..
,,	,,	5	17	Metal goods	S	..
Assistant General Manager	,,	5	342	Paper and board	M/L	M
GROUP 5. *Works Managers and Production Managers, in charge of one section of a large works*						
Production Manager	Middle	2	40	Food	L	M
Works Manager	Middle	11	1,150	Electrical machinery	L	..
Production Manager	,,	25	841	Chemical	L	..
Works Manager	,,	6	1,600	,,	L	..
,,	,,	5	1,000	Aircraft	L	..
Production Manager	,,	2	175	Chemical	L	..
,,	,,	4	115	,,	L	..
Production Control and Engineering Managers						
Production Control	,,	7	48	Heavy engineering	L	M
Factory Services	,,	5	132	Chemical	L	..
Director, Production Planning	Top	3	..	Steel	L	..
Technical Officer	Middle	..	..	Chemical	L	..
Works Engineer	,,	..	..	,,	L	..
Other						
Principal, Training School	,,	10	70	Electronics	L	..
Department Head Accounts	,,	8	150	Food	L	..

Appendix IV
Description of the Method used for Classifying the Managers into Job Types

by Nigel Howard

1. Introduction

In this appendix I give a relatively non-technical description of the method used to classify the managers into homogeneous groups. The method was described in a paper by me to the International Conference of Operational Research Societies in Cambridge, 1964.[1] It is further developed in an appendix to a sociological survey of London, prepared by the Centre for Urban Studies under the direction of Ruth Glass.[2] A review of classification methods is given in Sokal and Sneath, *Principles of Numerical Taxonomy*.[3] My particular method basically resembles that of Edwards and Cavalli-Sforza, 'A Method for Cluster Analysis', *Biometrics* (June 1965).[4]

2. Measure of Distance Between Two Objects

Consider two objects (such as managers), each of which is characterised by its set of values of a number of variables (such as the percentage of a manager's time spent in paperwork, in committee meetings and so on). If there were only three variables, each object could be represented geometrically as a point in three-dimensional space – the three coordinates of the space being the three variables. This is illustrated in Figure 1, where manager 1 works more hours and spends a greater percentage of his time on paperwork, but a lesser percentage in committees, than manager 2.

We might think of taking, as a measure of the overall difference in characteristics between these managers, the *distance* between them in this geometrical space. Better, we might take the *squared distance* – since this increases the effect of larger differences in particular variables, and hence helps to ensure, when we have more than two managers, that two managers who are considered *close* to each other are fairly close in practically every variable. However, it is clear that this requires that the units in which the variables are measured be commensurate in some way – otherwise, by increasing arbitrarily the length of a unit of one variable, and so stretching its axis, one could give that variable an arbitrarily great effect in determining the closeness of managers to each other. We get round this by taking as the unit

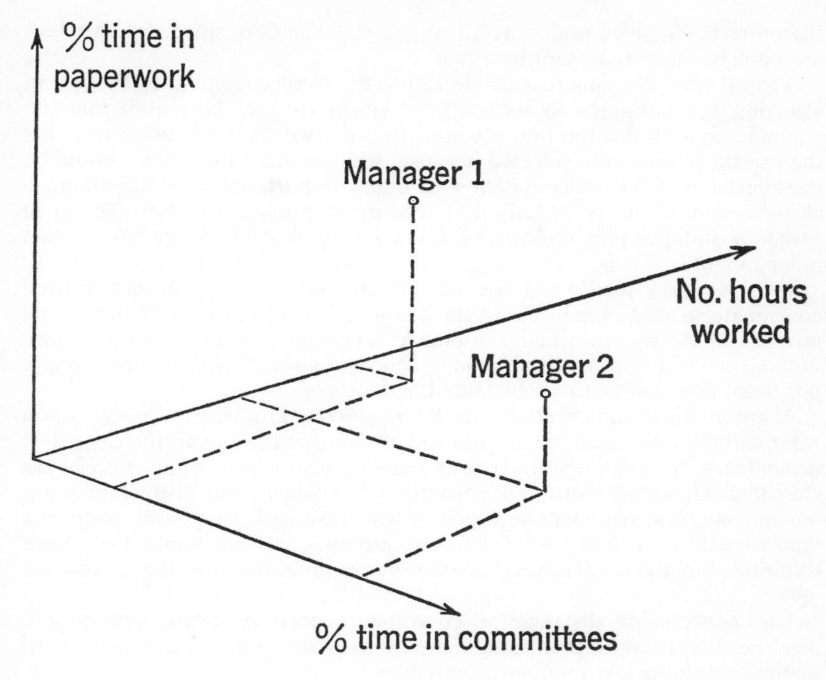

Figure 1

of each variable its *standard deviation* – which is a statistical measure of the degree to which the variable varies over the whole population of objects to be classified. This is called *standardising* the variables. When each variable is standardised, each varies over the population to the same extent as each other – its standard deviation being one.[5]

The expedient of standardisation is commonly used to make variables commensurate – though with little theoretical justification. However, one might justify it for the purpose of classifying by a number of incommensurable variables on these grounds. When variables are being selected initially to classify by, they must be intuitively compared in the process of estimating whether they should be selected or not; hence some method of making the variables commensurate must exist, intuitively, in the mind of the person making the selection. The method that the person thus has intuitively in mind may well be a method similar to standardisation – just as the concept of the 'average' member of a population is no doubt what an untrained person intuitively uses when he thinks of a 'typical member'.

Another point is this. Two variables used to classify by may not be *independent*. That is, there may be a tendency for a high value of one to accompany a high (or low) value of the other. In this case, their dependence may be due to the influence on both of some third variable – which is perhaps therefore being given undue weight in the classification, since two variables are being used to represent its effect.

Against this, it seems reasonable to use the same argument as before. In selecting the variables to be used, we may assume that intuitively the comparison took this too into account. In other words, we may assume that the variables used were selected because, when standardised, they would be considered to have independent and equal importance in determining a classification of the type desired. There is, of course, no contradiction in assigning independent *importance* to two variables which are not in fact independent.

Thus we may justify the use of the squared distance in standardised coordinate space as a measure of the dissimilarity between two objects – the purpose of the measure being to enable a classification of the objects into homogeneous groups to be obtained. This discussion, however, has brought out three points which may be stated as follows:

A multivariate classification into homogeneous groups will depend upon *what* variables are used, what *units* are chosen for them, and the degree of *dependence* between them. It will depend also upon what *objects* are classified. Hence, if a different selection of managers had been classified – having, say, few managers of a type of which we had many, and many of a type of which we had few – then the groups obtained would have been different. Finally, it will depend on *how many* groups the objects are classified into.

The concept of distance in coordinate space is easily generalised, algebraically, to more than three dimensions. And so we have a measure of dissimilarity over any number of variables.

3. Measure of Homogeneity of a Classification

Consider now a population which has been divided, in some way, into p groups. Each group will have a *mean* – that is, in geometrical space, it will have a centre of gravity, the coordinates of which will be the means, over the group, of each variable taken separately. The population of objects as a whole also has a mean (centre of gravity).

If now, within a group, we sum the square distances from each object to the mean, we have a measure of the *inhomogeneity* of that group. Summing these measures over all groups, we have a measure of the inhomogeneity of the whole classification.

This measure tells us how much the objects in each group resemble each other. But another criterion of homogeneity would be how much the objects in different groups differ from each other. Taking a group as represented by its mean, we might, in order to measure this, imagine that each object is replaced by an object at the mean of its group (so that the centre of gravity of each group becomes simultaneously occupied by all the objects in that group); and, after having done this, take the sum of squared distances between each pair of objects (now zero between objects in the same group) as a measure of the *homogeneity* of the classification.

It turns out that these two measures are in full agreement, for we can prove, when inhomogeneity and homogeneity are defined in this way, that, for any classification

Inhomogeneity of classification + Homogeneity of classification
= a Constant

Hence, since on the right we have a constant, we shall, by increasing the homogeneity of a classification automatically decrease its inhomogeneity by the same amount.

This formula is more commonly expressed by writing:

Total within-group variation + Total between-group variation
= Total variation

– the total variation being the sum of square distances of all objects to the mean of the whole population. It is the many-dimensional form of the basic equation of the Analysis of Variance – for which see Fisher, *Statistical Methods for Research Workers.*[6]

4. A Necessary Condition for an Optimal Classification

If we now seek an *optimal* classification into a fixed number p of groups – in the sense of a p-fold classification with minimum inhomogeneity or, equivalently, maximum homogeneity – we find ourselves faced with an enormous task. The number of different classifications to be tested, were we to test them all, is too large for the largest computer if the number of objects in the population is more than about 15. Moreover, since the classification obtained will vary with p, the number of groups, we should like to compare a number of classifications with different values of p – unless we can prejudge how many groups there ought to be. If, on the other hand, we approach the problem by starting with an *initial* classification and transferring objects one at a time between groups in such a way as always to bring about an improvement until no further improvement by this means is possible, we find that this will not guarantee that we shall finally reach the optimum.

However, it does guarantee that we shall reach a classification which fulfils the *necessary condition* for an optimum that it shall not be possible to transfer any single element in such a way as to increase the homogeneity. Moreover, it turns out that this necessary condition implies a certain valuable property – that each object is nearer to the mean of its own group than to the mean of any other. Thus each object may be said to be better represented by its own mean than by any other.

This, then, is the type of classification the computer finds. It is not necessarily optimal, but it has certain optimal properties.

But there may be more than one classification with these optimal properties. Of course, there may also be more than one optimal classification: but since the set of optimal classifications is a subset of the set with certain optimal properties, there will generally be more classifications with the optimal properties than there are optimal ones. So the question – what factors decide which one is obtained? – is that much more relevant.

The computer begins with an initial classification into p groups, which it then improves by single transfers until no further such improvement is possible. The end result may thus depend on the initial classification.

The initial classifications, for each p, were obtained as follows. First, a twofold initial classification was obtained by splitting the managers into two groups according to whether they scored above or below the mean in one variable, *a priori* the most important.[7] The variable chosen was the proportion of time spent with other people. The final two-classification was then found. Next, in general, the initial classification into p groups was found by splitting the groups of the final $(p-1)$-fold classification with the greatest total within variation into two groups according to the values of the variable with the greatest variation within that group.

It seems that in fact the initial classification, thus determined, did affect the final classifications for each p. Thus, there was a tendency for the p-fold classification to resemble its initial classification.

Next, the final classifications obtained may depend on the order in which the objects are considered by the computer. This dependence – which is unfortunate – could have been practically eliminated by transferring, at each stage, that object whose transfer would have most increased the homogeneity, but this was not done for reasons of economy in programming. As it is, there may be a tendency for objects earlier in the list to be better classified than later ones.

5. Tests of Significance

The computer output, then, consisted of 9 classifications in all – a classification into 2 groups, one into 3 groups, . . . and finally one into 10 groups. The question then arose – which classification was the most interesting or 'significant'?

No test of significance in the usual statistical sense was available, but certain more or less intuitively justifiable tests could be made.

(i) It is not a characteristic of the method used that the groups of the $(p+k)$-fold classification (k being positive) should be subsets of the p-fold classification. To the extent that this hierarchical relationship between two classifications in a sense embody the same principle of classification: for they group the objects in the same way, except that one goes into more detail (has more groups) than the other.

But this statement must be qualified. I mentioned in section 4 that the method is probably biased towards finding a hierarchical relationship between the p-fold and the $(p+1)$-fold classification. However, hierarchical relationships which appear to be stronger than this bias generally leads to may still be taken as indicating a principle of classification which is truly 'present in the data'.

Applying this to the classifications of the managers, it was found that the threefold classification and the classifications from the fivefold one onwards had all fairly strong hierarchical relationships with each other, but not on the whole with the twofold and the fourfold classifications – which were not either strongly related to each other. This pointed to the threefold and the fivefold classifications as being interesting ones.[8]

(ii) The *variance*, which is the square of the standard deviation mentioned already, is an alternative measure of the variation of a variable in a population or group. It has the property that a random sample from a population is expected to have much the same variance as the population itself. If, then, the *total variance* of each group in a classification (that is, the variance over that group of each variable, summed over all variables) is less than the total variance of the whole poplation, the classification might be considered a good one.

A criterion along these lines would be independent of the number of groups in the classification. In fact, it seems that a true test of significance might be built on it.

Against this, my argument is that the method of classification aims at maximising homogeneity, so that it would seem inappropriate to judge its results by any formal criterion other than the homogeneity obtained. This is discussed under (iii).

In any case, no group in the classifications had a greater total variance than the original population; and no classification appeared to be markedly better or worse than the others, judged by this criterion.

(iii) If we attempt to evaluate the classifications by the degree of their homogeneity – which was what the method attempted to maximise – we run up against a characteristic difficulty. This is that the greater the number of groups, the greater must be the homogeneity, so that this criterion would automatically lead us to the classification with the largest number of groups. In some way we must counter this and it is clear in principle how we should do it. A classification seeks to summarise the original data. The smaller the number of groups, the more compact the summary, but the greater the inhomogeneity, the less information will the summary contain. In principle, then, we should assign a utility to having p groups which should decrease with p, and a utility to homogeneity which should increase with the homogeneity; and if we could do this, a classification would exist which would give us maximum utility.

In practice, this assignment of utilities may not, as in this case, be possible. However, we can glean something from an examination of *how* the homogeneity increases as the number of groups is increased. In Table 2, the first column gives the number of groups, the second the homogeneity of the classification with that number of groups. The third column gives the difference between successive entries in the second column, and tells us that the homogeneity increases (as it must) with the number of groups, but on the whole at a decreasing rate. The fourth column, obtained by differencing the third, gives the increase in homogeneity from 'leaving' a classification *less* that from 'coming' to it – and thus affords a comparison between a classification and its two neighbours. It is worth while increasing the number of groups by one if the gain in homogeneity is large, not if it is not. Hence large negative entries in the last column indicate potentially interesting classifications.

The results again point to the threefold and the fivefold classifications.

Table 2 Behaviour of 'homogeneity' (percentage of between variation) as the number of groups increases from classification to classification

No of groups	*% between variation*	*1st differences*	*2nd differences*
1	0		
		10	
2	10		1
		11	
3	21		−8
		3	
4	24		3
		6	
5	30		−4
		2	
6	32		0
		2	
7	34		0
		2	
8	36		−1
		1	
9	37		1
		2	
10	39		

(iv) The final, and probably the most important, criterion for judging a classification is its interpretability, which is discussed in the text.

6. The Computer Program

The computer program is available for use at the University of London Atlas Computing Service, 44 Gordon Square, London, W.C.1, from whom more information on it may be obtained.

LIST OF THE TWENTY-FIVE VARIABLES USED FOR THE CLASSIFICATION INTO JOB TYPES

Each manager was classified on the basis of his score for the four weeks on each of the variables. The variables were given equal weight.

1. Total hours worked.
2. Total number of entries.
3. Total number of fleeting contacts.
4. Percentage of total time spent alone.
5. with one other person.
6. with two or more other people.
7. in his own establishment (not including time spent in other units of the company).
8. outside the company.
9. in travelling.
10. with his boss.
11. with his secretary.
12. with his immediate subordinates.
13. with his subordinates' subordinates.
14. with his colleagues.
15. with his fellow-specialists.
16. with other internal contacts.
17. with customers.
18. with suppliers.
19. with other external contacts.
20. in committees.
21. in all other forms of discussion.
22. in all forms of paperwork.
23. in inspection.
24. spent on personnel matters.
25. spent on the four headings of the 'What?' column which took least time, excluding general management. (This was included as a guide to the range of management functions with which the manager was concerned.)

Notes

Introduction to the First Edition

1. The word 'manager' is used in many different ways, but there are two main distinctions. The first uses the word 'manager' to cover all those above a certain level in the hierarchy, usually those above foreman level on the works side and those above the first level of supervision in the offices. The second uses 'manager' in a more restricted sense for all above a certain level, again usually foreman, who have subordinates and therefore manage other people directly. It is used in the first sense in this book. The term 'executive' is often, though not universally, used in the USA when referring to senior managers. It is also sometimes used in that way in the UK. Because there is no consistent usage, it was decided to use the word 'manager' throughout the book. Most of the discussion is about the work of middle and senior managers.

1 Studying What Managers Do

1. T. Burns, 'Management in Action', *Operational Research Quarterly*, vol. viii, no. 2 (June 1957) pp. 45–60; T. A. Mahoney, J. H. Jerdee and S. J. Carroll, *Development Managerial Performance: A Research Approach*, Monograph C-9 (South-Western Publishing, USA, 1963); Sune Carlson, *Executive Behaviour: A Study of the Workload and Working Methods of Managing Directors* (Stockholm: Strombergs, 1951); Ralph M. Stogdill, Carroll L. Shartle *et al.*, *Patterns of Administrative Performance* (Ohio State University, Bureau of Business Research, Monograph no. 81, 1956) p. 48.
2. Ralph M. Stogdill, C. Shartle, E. Scott, A. E. Coons and W. E. Jaynes, *A Predictive Study of Administrative Work Patterns* (Ohio State University, Bureau of Business Research, Monograph no. 85, 1956).
3. More information about these experiments in methods of recording is given in Rosemary Stewart, 'The Use of Diaries to Study Managers' Jobs', *The Journal of Management Studies*, vol. ii, no. 2 (May 1965) pp. 228–35.

2 How the Managers Spent their Time

1. T. Burns, 'Management in Action', *Operational Research Quarterly*, vol. viii, no. 2 (June 1957) p. 48.
2. J. H. Horne and Tom Lupton, 'The Work Activities of "Middle" Managers', *The Journal of Management Studies*, vol. i, no. 2 (February 1965) p. 30.
3. Incomes Data Services Ltd, *Hours and Holidays 1986*, Study 372 (October 1986).

4. David Norburn, *British Corporate Leaders – A Profile* (London: Korn Ferry International, 1981).
5. Burns, 'Management in Action', p. 48.
6. Ibid.
7. Joan Woodward, *Industrial Organization: Theory and Practice* (Oxford: OUP, 1965) p. 67.
8. Rosemary Stewart, *Choices for the Manager* (Maidenhead: McGraw-Hill (UK), 1982, and Englewood Cliffs: Prentice-Hall, 1982).
9. In retrospect it would have been better to provide an additional category for pre-arranged pair discussions rather than including them under 'Informal discussions'.

3 Other People

1. A manager who was on the telephone for five minutes or longer was classified as being with one other person. Shorter telephone calls, and face-to-face discussions of under five minutes, were included in the time spent alone if they took place when the manager was working on his own. These brief discussions were considered as interruptions of the time when the manager was alone. This is discussed in the next chapter, where allowance is made for the reduction in the managers' time alone. Figure 3.1 includes these brief contacts.
2. The odds against the differences between the two groups being due to chance are more than 100:1.

4 No Time to Think

1. All names used in this book are fictitious.

5 Variety within Jobs

1. 'Six Senior Hospital Administrators Studied by Six Junior Hospital Administrators', unpublished report 1965.

6 Job Profiles

1. In later research the author developed classifications for some aspects of managerial work. See Rosemary Stewart, *Contrasts in Management: A Study of Different Types of Managers' Jobs, their Demands and Choices* (Maidenhead: McGraw Hill (UK) 1976).
2. For details of the individual managers in each group see Appendix III.

7 Implications of Job Types

1. The nature of contacts in terms of who the manager has to deal with, and the factors affecting the difficulty of the relationship, were analysed in a later study, Rosemary Stewart, *Contrasts in Management*.

8 What *Do* Managers Do?

1. Rosemary Stewart, *Contrasts in Management*.
2. J. H. Horne and Tom Lupton, 'The Work Activities of "Middle" Managers'.
3. T. Burns, 'Management in Action', pp. 45–60.
4. Horne and Lupton, 'The Work Activities of "Middle" Managers', p. 32.
5. Leonard R. Sayles, *Administration in Complex Organizations* (New York: McGraw-Hill, 1964) p. 258.
6. John P. Kotter, *The General Managers* (New York: The Free Press, 1982).
7. Henry Mintzberg, *The Nature of Managerial Work* (New York: Harper & Row, 1973).
8. Karl E. Weick, 'Managerial Thought in the Context of Action', in Suresh Srivasta *et al., The Executive Mind* (San Francisco: Jossey-Bass, 1983) p. 238.
9. The idea of the effective manager as the opportunistic manager is one of the most useful contributions to thinking about the implications of what managers do. It is discussed in both Mintzberg, *The Nature of Managerial Work*, p. 181, and Kotter, *The General Managers*, pp. 88–91.
10. Carlson, *Executive Behaviour*, p. 62.
11. Mintzberg, *The Nature of Managerial Work*, pp. 178–9.
12. Carlson, *Executive Behaviour*, p. 70.
13. The extent of choice that exists in managerial jobs and the implications of this for improving managerial effectiveness, and potentially for enjoying one's job more, are discussed in Rosemary Stewart, *Choices for the Manager*.

9 Too Little Time? How to Help Yourself

1. H. Luijk, in G. Copeman, H. Luijk and F. de P. Hanika, *How the Executive Spends his Time* (London: Business Publications, 1963) p. 73.
2. Carlson, *Executive Behaviour*, pp. 66–7.
3. C. N. Parkinson, *Parkinson's Law and Other Studies in Administration* (Boston, Massachusetts: Houghton Mifflin, 1957).

Appendix IV: Description of the Method used for Changing the Managers into Job Types (Nigel Howard)

1. R. N. Howard, 'Classifying a Population into Homogeneous Groups'; in J. R. Lawrence (ed.), *Operational Research and the Social Sciences* (London: Tavistock, 1966) pp. 585–94.
2. Ruth Glass (ed.), *The Third Survey of London Life and Labour,* vol. 1: *The Socio-geographical Pattern* (London: Weidenfeld & Nicolson, 1967).

3. R. R. Sokal and P. H. A. Sneath, *Principles of Numerical Taxonomy* (San Francisco: W. H. Freeman, 1963).
4. A. W. F. Edwards and L. L. Cavalli-Sforza, 'A Method for Cluster Analysis', *Biometrics*, vol. xxi, no. 2 (June 1965).
5. The standard deviation of a variable is defined as

$$\sqrt{\frac{1}{n}\left((x_1-\bar{x})^2+(x_2-\bar{x})^2+\ldots+(x_n-\bar{x})^2\right)},$$

where n is the number of objects in the population, x_1 is the value of the variable for the ith object, and $\bar{x}$ is the mean value for the population.
6. R. A. Fisher, *Statistical Methods for Research Workers* (Edinburgh: Oliver & Boyd, 1954).

Index